Characteristics
and
Dynamics
of
Incest
and
Child Sexual Abuse

by Tony Martens

with

A Native Perspective

by
Brenda Daily
and
Maggie Hodgson

Published by: Nechi Institute
                     P.O. Box 2039 Stn Main
                     St. Albert, AB
                     T8N 1M9
                     CANADA
                     (Phone 403-458-1884)

Book Design and Layout: Wordsmith Communications

Cover Illustration: Terry McCue

"The Secret Loser" with permission of Nadine Callihoo Oshanyk

Canadian Cataloguing in Publication Data

Martens, Tony, 1956-
    Characteristics and dynamics of incest and child sexual abuse

Cover title: The spirit weeps.
Includes biographical references.
ISBN 0-9693440-2-3
Fourth Printing 1997

1. Incest. 2. Child abuse. 3. Child molesting. 4. Indians of North America. I. Daily, Brenda, 1948- II. Hodgson, Maggie, 1944- III. Nechi Institute on Alcohol and Drug Education. IV. Title. V. Title: The spirit weeps.
HQ71.M37 1991   362.7′4   091-091206-8

Printed and Bound in Canada

My Story

I was once a young child, although I find it very hard to remember the time. When I look back it seems that I grew up so quickly. The fears that I had were plenty. The stories that my friends tell me of their childhood and growing up years I cannot relate to. It's strange, oh so strange, because neither can they. Although we are of the same age, our experiences were so different. They tell me it's hard for them to accept mine, but as I assure them, it is not as difficult as it is for me to accept it.

I've been asked many times, since my growing up years, what it would have taken for me to stop and change the direction of my life. I believe that is easy for me to answer. All I would have needed back then was to feel loved and trusted. All I would have needed was for someone to hold me and care for me, and most of all, someone to believe in me.

Nothing more than that.

"Sharon"

Contents

Foreword

Currently as awareness about family violence and child sexual abuse grows, many questions are being asked about what these issues mean as they relate to Native people. These questions dovetail with questions about Native people in general. Some of these include:

Is violence and sexual abuse different in Native country?

Do Native people have a cultural norm of violence and abuse?

Was or is, incest culturally acceptable?

Can Native people find the answers to their problems by going back to their traditional ways?

Unfortunately, we are at a stage where little written information exists about Natives and these subjects. It is my belief that there are both similarities and differences between what we see in the white world and what we see in the Native world. Our greatest challenge is in clarifying and defining these.

I also believe that abuse is abuse, and all individuals experience pain if they are subjected to abuse or are abusing others. I think that Natives and non-Natives have a great deal to learn from one another, and there is no robbery in fair exchange. This manual was written with the intention of exploration and trade between two cultures in mind. Knowledge about sexual abuse and treatment is offered from a rural program that operates in the white world. Native people have been successfully treated within this program. I suspect that the program could be modified and adapted to serve a Native community; it provides a model for advocacy and hope.

Tony Martens' descriptions of families suffering from child sexual abuse and incest is based on his knowledge and experience as a director and therapist within this program, and more than 10 years experience counselling sexual abuse victims. To his material, I have added notes and footnotes which help to clarify some Native aspects of the issues he is discussing. Our experience tells us that many of the dynamics of incestuous families are the same among Natives and non-Natives.

In a separate chapter I explore specific Native aspects of the problem and the historical context from which they have evolved. In the final chapter, Maggie Hodgson further describes some factors to consider in designing programs to deal with incest and sexual abuse in Native communities.

It is our hope that caring individuals will persevere in the search for solutions to these problems as they affect Native people, and that the information in this book will assist them in that search.

This is not a "how-to" manual; nor is the material intended to be prescriptive in pointing out specific interventions. Because of the vast differences in resources available to various communities, regions and jurisdictions, it would be misleading to say there is a definite set of rules or procedures that one can follow in treating Native families.

In beginning the struggle to break the cycle of abuse, however, knowledge and consideration seem to be a good place to start.

Brenda Daily
Edmonton, Alberta

Acknowledgements

There are so many people whose contributions to this book must be recognized. First of all, I'd like to thank the victims of incest, their siblings, non-offending parents, and the offenders who permitted me to use their letters and comments made in therapy.

I would also like to thank Health Canada, for providing the funds which made possible the production of this book, Brenda Daily and Maggie Hodgson for their valuable contributions, and Terry McCue for his beautiful cover illustration.

My appreciation also, to Jim Taylor for his patience in reviewing and editing the separate contributions, and putting all the parts together.

Finally, and most of all, I thank my families: my parents for raising me in a loving home free of abuse; and my wife Susan, and children, Christine and Jason, for allowing me the extended time needed for writing the book.

Tony Martens
Hinton, Alberta
July, 1988

I would like to acknowledge my Brothers and Sisters working in the addictions field, the ongoing spirit of my father, Ben Daily, who taught me the meaning of courage and kindness, and my sons Monty, Clark, and Jordan.

Brenda Daily
Edmonton, Alberta
July, 1988

Thank you, Joe Couture, for your guidance in my spiritual development, to my husband, Don, for being willing to walk with me in my journey, and to the Indian Community who honored trust.

Maggie Hodgson
Edmonton, Alberta
July, 1988

Chapter 1
Introduction

What type of man would sexually assault children, and what kind of woman would continue to live with him? Why doesn't a child who is being abused simply tell someone? If she keeps silent about the abuse, does that mean she enjoys the incestuous relationship? Whose fault is it when incest occurs? What about boys; are they ever sexually abused? And what about women; are they ever the abusers?

These are just a few of the questions that are asked by people who are struggling to find solutions to the complex problem of incest and child sexual abuse. This manual attempts to answer these and other questions, and give readers an improved understanding of the dynamics of sexually abusive families.

Increasing public awareness of the problem has led many people to believe that incest in society is a relatively new problem, but it is not; literature reveals that incest goes back as far as time itself. What is new, however, is people's willingness to speak openly about the problem, and address the issues surrounding it. Along with this has come an increase, in recent decades, in reports of incest and child sexual abuse. Again, this should not be taken as evidence that incest or child sexual abuse is occurring more frequently than in the past; it shows only that it is being reported more often.

This new openness is not without its detractors. Some people fear that open discussions pertaining to incest and child sexual abuse will be harmful and cause confusion among individuals and families; there is, after all, no universal agreement about what is appropriate sexual contact between people, and what is inappropriate. The most universal cultural taboo about incest and child sexual abuse is not primarily that these acts do not occur; rather it is against discussing such matters.*

We believe, however, that increased understanding of the problem is a vital component to solving it. Incest is not a "private family matter"; it is a social issue and the common good is truly at stake. The way people see themselves and the lives that they lead contribute to or detract from society. Many prostitutes, runaways and young offenders report abusive backgrounds. Heightened awareness of incest and child sexual abuse will help lessen the problem, creating a healthier society in the future.

In some Native families discussing any sexual matters between certain members of the family was taboo. For instance, it would have been frowned upon, at the least, or even totally unacceptable to have a son-in-law and mother-in-law in the same room during a discussion about sexuality.

Many people know very little about incest and child sexual abuse, and even less about its dynamics and characteristics. Their viewpoints have been shaped by sensationalized media reports from newspapers, magazines and television.*

As a result, they often express judgements and prejudices which are based on very little accurate information. **(See Figure 1)**

It is our desire that this manual will help to alleviate some of the misconceptions and misunderstandings about the individuals and families where incest and child sexual abuse has occurred. With a clearer understanding of why it has occurred, professionals and society as a whole will be better equipped to help break the cycle of abuse.

In order to understand the dynamics of an incestuous family, it is necessary to look at the smallest components of that family, the individuals within it. We have done this by discussing the victim, the offender, the non-offending parent and the siblings, each in turn. We have described the characteristics of each person and the dynamics of his/her role within the family. Included will be actual accounts of individuals in an incestuous/child abusive family. (The names have all been changed, of course, to protect the privacy of the people involved.)

We have also included information pertaining to others whose influence on the incestuous family is significant, the parents of both the offender and the non-offending parent.

The information presented here is based on years of clinical research and thousands of hours of therapy to hundreds of individuals who have experienced and/or committed incest or child sexual abuse.

Notes to Helpers

Our experience shows us that many people who seek to work in the field of incest and child sexual abuse are, themselves, the victims of abusive backgrounds. They seek the role of helper as a means of resolving their own past issues.

If this describes you, may we suggest that you must first deal with the problems of your own past before you can be effective in helping others. If you attempt to assist others without coming to terms with your own pain, you may do more harm than good, in spite of your best intentions. **(See Figure 2)** You will also find your own pain compounded, and may end up feeling angry, isolated, powerless, ineffective and burnt out. You must take care of yourself before and while you help others to address their needs.

Many northern communities have been introduced to television only in recent years and have been dramatically impacted by it. Some communities have reported the affect of "blue" movies; young men have asked their partners to do the things they have seen on television.

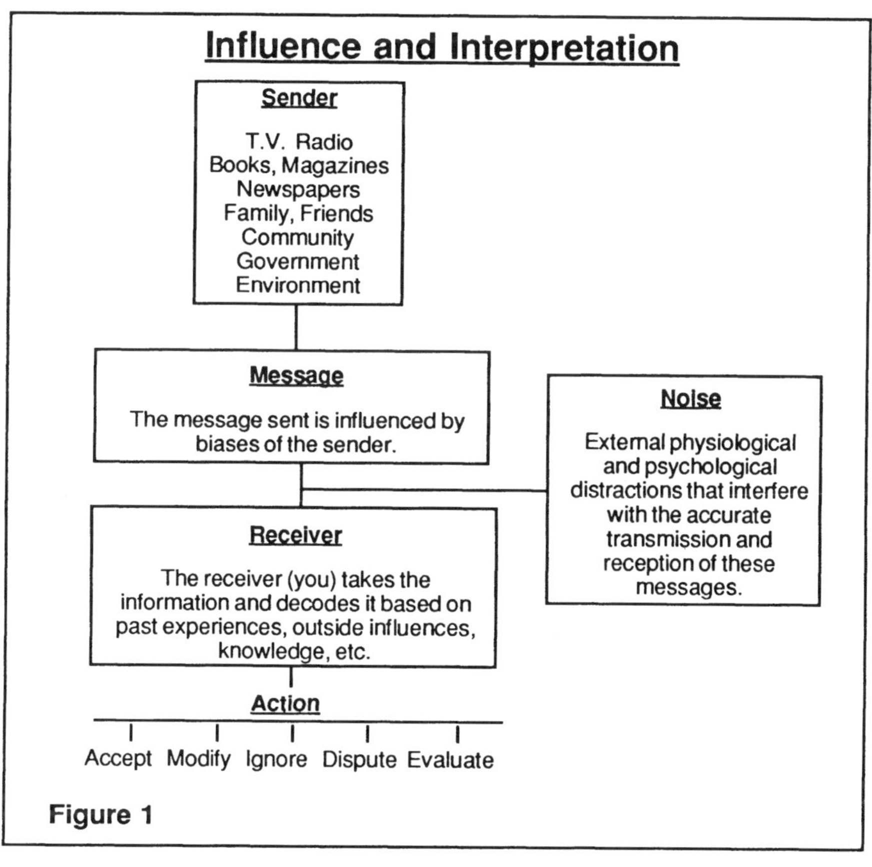

Figure 1

The Process of Helping

1. Evaluate your own past experiences and address issues of conflict and traumatization.

2. Assess your own beliefs, values, and morals in order to understand why you make certain choices and do what you do in life.

3. Assess whether or not you have come to terms with the issues of those you are assisting, prior to assisting them. These issues relate to power, sexuality, families and sex roles.

4. Continually assess your own life and ask yourself whether or not you practice what you preach.

Figure 2

Whether or not you are a victim of past sexual abuse, it is essential for you to evaluate your own values and belief structure, and assess your background. Helpers are, after all, subject to the same influences which shape the lives of people in general.

Throughout our lives, our experiences and what we are taught tend to point out a direction which each of us follows. We grow up, live and do the things which confirm to us the image we have of ourselves and others; we focus on situations, circumstances and happenings that validate our own perceptions.

Even if these perceptions are unjustly biased, we often try to justify them and rationalize them to fit and suit our own needs. If the needs we are attempting to fulfill are unhealthy, then the manner in which we affirm our perception of self could be damaging not only to ourselves, but to others as well.

Therefore, in order to help others, you need to address issues from your past that are unresolved. Only by dealing with these personal issues, can you be effective in understanding and helping those people whose lives have been traumatized by incest or child sexual abuse.

A Final Word of Caution

While we hope to improve the ability of potential helpers to assist families experiencing abuse, we would like to emphasize that reading this manual does not qualify one to offer therapy.

Notes:

In the pages which follow, we have often used "she" and "her" as pronouns for the victim or non-offending spouse, and "he" and "him" for the offender. We are not suggesting that the victims of incest or sexual abuse are always female and the offenders male; both victims and offenders can be of either sex. For reasons of grammatical simplicity, however, we chose these pronouns when speaking in general terms, because they do reflect the most common case. When dealing with specific cases, we have identified the gender of the individuals involved, and their relationship to each other.

The quotations from therapy sessions, and personal letters printed in this book, have been transcribed verbatim as accurately as possible, without changes to the original grammar.

Chapter 2
Myths About Incest and Child Sexual Abuse

Often people's opinions and perceptions about incest and child sexual abuse are based on myths and misconceptions. Some of these are described below. In understanding the problem, it is also important to understand the specific meanings of each of the terms used. Therefore, please refer to the Glossary for definitions.

Myth: Incest offenders are insane, oversexed, or pedophiles.

In reality, none of these charges is generally true. Research indicates that incest offenders are usually not psychotic and do not suffer from mental illness.

Neither are they "oversexed"; their main motivation is not a desire to satisfy sexual needs. An offender may receive some sexual satisfaction from the acts he commits, but his primary gratification is the sense of power, control and domination he feels when assaulting his victim.

Therefore, even though a man may be involved sexually with his own child, it is not correct to assume that he is a pedophile; his primary sexual attraction may be towards women of his own age.

Another error would be to assume that only homosexuals assault members of their own sex. Since the main motive of offenders is to achieve control and domination rather than sexual gratification, heterosexual men may sexually assault boys in order to exercise this power and control.

In general, incest and child sexual abuse is perpetrated by people who know the victim and are usually in a position of trust or power over them. They commit their assaults not in isolated woods or playgrounds, but often in the child's own home or other places where the child feels safe.

Myth: Males are not usually sexually abused.

Reports of males being victimized sexually are less frequent than those of females, but we know that boys too, are victims of incest and child sexual abuse. Because of the stigma placed on males who report sexual abuse, most find it very difficult to expose these acts. If a male has been sexually assaulted by another male, he tends to view this act as homosexual and fears that others would see him as being gay. As a result, many abused boys do not disclose.

Unfortunately, investigations conducted into sexual abuse or incest within a family often overlook the possibility that the males within the family may have been sexually assaulted.* Helpers involved in investigating incestuous families should be alert to the possibility that the boys within the family have also been sexually assaulted or otherwise abused.

Myth: If no force is used, incest and child sexual abuse is not violent.

Acts of incest and child sexual abuse themselves define violence. These are acts of aggression, domination, coersion, manipulation and self-seeking with no regard for the damage done to the victim. Although the perpetrator may not use physical force, and may even appear to be loving and caring, the emotional traumatization created through the destruction of trust and exertion of power has a violent, devastating effect on the victim. This damages the child's self-esteem and self concept.

Furthermore, one cannot assume that a particular form of sexual contact is more or less traumatic for the child than some other form, for example that masturbation is more traumatic than fondling. The degree of trauma experienced by the child as a result of any form of abuse is entirely situational.

In treating victims of sexual abuse or incest, the primary issue that is addressed is not the sexual act, but rather the emotional injury that has resulted from it.

Myth: Incest occurs only in lower class families.

Incest spans all social, economic, racial and cultural boundaries. Often people in the lower economic brackets are able to reach out and ask for assistance if they are involved with agencies or organizations where disclosure could take place. This indicates only that people in this group may be disclosing and seeking assistance more often than people in other social-economic brackets, or that they are more highly monitored by helping agencies like Social Services. It does *not* mean that incest or sexual abuse occurs more often in this group.

Myth: Most child victims willingly go along with the sexual acts, or even want to be involved with an adult.

Child victims believe they have no choice as to whether they go along with the sexual acts or not. Through the offender's ability to manipulate and coerce, most children do not initially understand what is happening. If a child has perceived the sexual

Many Native males have been sexually abused in institutional settings such as jail, foster care and residential schools.

involvement with the offender as an acknowledgement of love and caring, at times they may seek this out. The perpetrator may interpret the child's behavior as seductive and encouraging the relationship, but this is not true.

Children whose behavior could be seen as "seductive" are not seeking out sexual exploitation or touching, but an acknowledgement that they are accepted, needed and cared for. Sexual "acting out" behavior is learned through the manipulation of the offender.

Myth: Children fabricate allegations of incest and child sexual abuse.

There is no evidence to substantiate that children generally lie about allegations of incest or child sexual abuse; there may be exceptions to this, but false allegations are extremely rare.

On the contrary, children are much more likely to withhold information about sexual abuse that has occurred, than invent abuse that has not. For example, if intercourse has taken place, quite often children will deny that it has. They may have felt very dirty, degraded or "damaged" by it, or they may have reacted with a sexual response of their own and as a result feel guilty and responsible. During an investigation they may withhold this information for fear that disclosure may incriminate them.

Frequently children retract either part or all of their statements pertaining to allegations of abuse. It would be an error for people in authority or the public at large to view these retractions as an admission that the initial allegations were false. Children retract their statements for a multitude of reasons, the least likely of which is that the initial allegations were fabricated.

Myth: There is usually only one child abused in an incestuous family.

The number of children sexually abused in an incestuous family depends on several factors. The offender needs to receive some sense of power, control or domination over the child in order to continue the sexual assaults.

For example, if a father offender has four children, two male and two female, and all the children are very withdrawn and submissive with no real sense of self, he will quite likely assault more than one, if not all of them. The children themselves, however, may not realize that their siblings are being sexually assaulted.

On the other hand, if two of the children in such a family appear aggressive and have a fairly well developed sense of self that would allow them to disclose the sexual abuse, the perpetrator is unlikely to sexually assault them for fear of disclosure and being revealed.

Even if these children are not *sexually* abused, however, they are still growing up in a dysfunctional family which provides an unhealthy, abusive environment for all the members of it. They too are victimized by the offender's problems pertaining to power, control and domination. The offender usually will treat the siblings he is not sexually abusing in a manner which creates distance, lack of trust and poor self-esteem.

The emotional abuse suffered by siblings of an incest victim results in traumatization that may be equal to that suffered by the victim.

Myth: Incest is usually a one-time occurrence.

It is usually quite rare to discover incest and/or child sexual abuse after the first incident as many victims are sexually assaulted at a very young age. They usually don't disclose until their teenage years, if ever. As a result they are usually sexually assaulted repeatedly, and often by more than one offender. Because the perpetrators typically have little understanding as to why they are sexually assaulting children, they usually are unable to stop after the first assault. Their sexually abusive behavior continues until a crisis of some kind prevents further abuse.

Myth: The stigma of sexual abuse is placed only on the offender and never on the child.

Frequently, children who have been victimized by sexual abuse are stigmatized as a result of the abuse. Often they lose friends and are told not to associate with certain peers. Victims are sometimes seen as being responsible for the sexual abuse occurring. In their teen-age years, they may develop behaviors (such as promiscuity) which raise questions about their character.

Myth: The non-offending parent in an incestuous family has no idea that sexual abuse is occurring.

In many cases, the non-offending spouse (usually the mother) in an incestuous family either knows or has some idea that the relationship between her child and husband is sexual or unhealthy. In some cases, the child has even gone to her and disclosed the sexual abuse.

Although she may not take any noticeable action upon suspecting or learning that sexual abuse is occurring, the inaction is often a result of not knowing how to deal with the situation, rather than of condoning or supporting it.

Myth: The child victim hates the offender and wants to be away from him.

It is not correct to assume that just because sexual abuse is occurring that the child despises the offender. On the contrary, the child usually knows and loves the offender and desires not to be away from this person, but only to have the abuse stop; she hates the abuse, but loves the abuser. This combination of feelings is painful and confusing.

Myth: Pregnancy due to an incestuous relationship will result in a mentally retarded child.

Rarely is a child, conceived in an incestuous relationship, born mentally retarded. However, if the incestuous relationships are multigenerational, the likelihood of birth defects increases.

Myth: Incest is, or was, a cultural norm in some Native societies.

There is no evidence to support this assertion. Legends which speak of incest are often subject to ethnocentric literal interpretations.

For instance, within a brother-sister, mother-son relationship it is important to ponder the difference in relationship concepts in Native societies. An animal, a rock or a tree can be regarded as a brother or a sister, if one has a spiritual connection with it. Stories are also used in healing or as psychological tools. Often a story is told to bleed off tension or as a device for individuals to address taboos.

Through the clash between two cultures, the disruption caused by assimilation and the entrance of alcohol into Native society, there was a breakdown in the social fabric which maintained order. Incest began to occur where it had never been seen before. Some Native communities are suffering from the third generation of incest. This is sometimes interpreted as acceptance or a cultural norm.

Myth: Alcohol and drug abuse cause sexually abusive behavior.

Substance abuse and sexual abuse are two separate behaviors which overlap each other. Individuals with both problems need treatment for both sets of behaviors, but each kind of treatment has separate and distinct goals.

Myth: A person with a history of sexual abuse is destined to become an abuser of his own children.

While it is true that most sexual abusers were themselves

victimized sexually or emotionally when they were children, this does not mean that they will necessarily become abusers of their own children. Many people experience some form of traumatization throughout their lives, and do not go on to abuse other people.

Chapter 3
Characteristics of a
Child Sexual Abuse Victim

Introduction

Although it is impossible to come up with one profile that describes all victims of incest and child sexual abuse, most of them share certain distinctive characteristics. These characteristics, however, may also apply to victims of other forms of abuse as well, such as physical or emotional abuse.

This section, first describes the wide range of psychological characteristics of incest and child sexual abuse victims, and then the similarly wide range of behavioral symptoms which they produce.

Psychological Characteristics

Low Self-Esteem

Self-esteem, the degree of regard that each person holds for himself or herself, is severely impaired in most child sexual abuse victims. This results from the sexual offender's deliberate efforts to control, and from the victim being forced to deny her basic needs on an ongoing basis. In the dysfunctional incestuous family, it is impossible for the victim to develop healthy self-esteem when she perceives that the members of her family treat her as worthless and not deserving of respect. Most sexually abused children come from such backgrounds and consequently develop low self-esteem and negative self images. Consider the self-esteem of the male child sexual abuse victim who wrote the following letter:

Dear Dad,

It's been a long time since I've ever said hello to you. I've been asked to write you a letter to explain to you a number of things that have been bothering me over the years. When I was young you used to make me feel as if I wasn't capable of doing anything right. You used to speak to me as if I was nobody. I remember so many times when you would act as if I wasn't even there. It would seem like days would pass and you wouldn't even talk to me. If it wasn't for mom I would have felt like I didn't belong to this family. When I was growing up I can remember when I needed to talk to you, but you acted like the things I had to say didn't matter at all. You used to get really mad at me when I did something wrong, but I can't remember you ever trying to teach me to do things right. I wished that we could have spent more time together when I was young, but I don't really think you ever wanted to do anything with me. When I was young, Dad, you would tell me that I had to be strong, and that if I cried it meant that I was weak. As a result, Dad, I didn't ever cry. Not even when mom died. I've been told that in the future you and I will probably have to talk a lot about these things. If we do get together, I hope that you will finally sit down and listen to what I have to say to you and not shut me out.

> *So long for now,*
> *Brian*

In his letter, Brian displays a sense of worthlessness with a supporting self image. What is especially interesting, in addition to the fact that Brian is a male victim, is that he was 35 years old when he wrote this letter. He was a past victim of sexual abuse by an uncle and by a number of female babysitters. I was working with him in treatment because he himself had sexually abused his two daughters over a period of approximately 3 years.

Here is another example, a letter written by a 14 year old boy who was sexually assaulted by his father and his aunt for approximately 3 years.

Dear Dad,
I'm not sure what I'm supposed to write to you in this letter, but I think I have a number of things to tell you. When mom and you would fight about me and Kathy, it made me feel as if I was to blame for everything that went wrong in this family. You never seemed to care about Kathy or I, and you never really treated mom very good either. You didn't seem to care when I did things right, but if I screwed up, that sure got your attention. I think that the only time you ever really talked to me was when I was in trouble. Maybe that's why I always got into trouble. When you started sexually abusing me and Kathy, we hated you. Mom was really scared of you, so we could never tell her about anything that you were doing because you probably would have beat her up. I think that I was stupid to have believed you when you told me that what you were doing was o.k. and that I wasn't supposed to tell anyone. You know I should have told somebody sooner. I'm not going to write any more right now. I'll wait until I see you face to face.

> *Kevin*

As you can see, the feelings and thoughts expressed by Kevin
are very similar to those of Brian. One more example, a letter
from a 14 year old female incest victim further illustrates this
point: it doesn't matter if the victim is young or old, male or
female, sexual abuse and incest create feelings of low self esteem
and negative self-image.

Dear Dad,

*Even thinking about writing you this letter makes me feel bad
inside. I will have to force myself to stop from getting mad at you.
I was told that it was o.k. for me to get mad at you because if that
is the way I feel then that is right for me, especially at this time.
But if I start I am afraid that I won't be able to stop myself from
saying so much hurtful things to you. It seems that part of me
wants to cry because of what you did to me, the other part of me
wants to cry for you. It's really confusing and scary. I think that
I've got to tell you what's on my mind even if it does hurt a little.
You confused me dad, when you made me believe that you were
touching me because mom treated you so bad. I talked to mom
now and she told me that it was you who didn't show love to her. I
just don't know who to believe anymore. Why does all this have to
be so complicated? Why did you ever have to do this to me?
Sometimes I wish that I could just crawl into a hole and die, and
I'm not just saying that to scare you either. You seem to never
believe me about anything that I was saying. I told you the truth
most of the time, but after a while I knew that you wouldn't believe
me, so I said whatever came to my mind. I had to lie about what
you were doing to me, so I may as well lie about everything else in
my life. I'm just starting to get mad at you, so I better end this
letter. But I just want you to know that I can still make something
out of my life and you can't stop me.*

Goodbye,
Cindy

Guilt

Most child sexual abuse victims have a strong sense of guilt.
Often they believe they are responsible for the sexual acts that
have occurred, that there is something about them, their bodies,
mannerisms or dress, that makes them responsible for the abuse.
This sense of guilt may prevent them from disclosing the abuse
out of fear that others will hold them responsible.

The victim's sense of guilt over the abuse is a characteristic
which is often deliberately cultivated and fostered by the sexual
offender, who fears that the child will disclose the abuse unless
she feels guilty about it. Through fault-finding and blaming the

child for problems in the family, the offender may start building up this sense of guilt well before he starts to sexually touch the victim. By breaking down the victim's sense of self-esteem and self concept, he creates a very insecure, easily dominated person, as is evidenced by the following excerpt.

"When I was first told that I wasn't responsible for what my dad did to me, I just couldn't believe it. I thought that there must have been something that I had done that made my dad want to do that to me. I remember I used to walk around the house with a real skimpy T-shirt on, and I thought for the longest time maybe that's what it was that made him want to touch me sexually. I was told that that's not true and that my dad wanted to control and dominate me more than anything else. That's beginning to make sense to me. Because some of my friends walk around the same way, and their fathers don't do that to them. When I look back before my dad started touching me, I remember that I was blamed for everything that went wrong in the family. I really thought that it was my responsibility whether or not the family stayed together because all the time my mom and dad told me that I was responsible for everything. I felt so guilty when they would argue and fight that I didn't know what to do. The biggest thing that I felt guilty about, and this may sound really dumb, is that I thought I was responsible to make my dad feel better. When he didn't feel better, I felt guilty about that. So sometimes what I would do would be to rub his back down and maybe pay attention to him, but when I did, it usually turned into sex. I felt guilty that he felt bad at the start, and then after he touched me sexually, I felt guilty because I thought I led him on. It was really so confusing for me. I just didn't know how to deal with it."

Pseudomaturity

Many child victims of sexual abuse exhibit pseudomaturity (a false sense of maturity), often as a result of role reversal. Frequently in an incestuous family, the child victim ends up "parenting" the parents. **(See Figure 3)** This can happen in respect to both the offender and non-offending parent(s).

In the case of the offender, the sexual activity between himself and the child tends to create a sense of premature development and a preoccupation with the sexual relationship which is confusing and disorienting to the child. This role confusion increases the likelihood that the sexual abuse or incest will continue, and creates a sense of responsibility and guilt on the part of the victim.

Role-reversal also occurs between the incest victims and their mothers. Consider the following experience described by a victim in therapy:

"It was like I was my mom's mom. I don't know if you can understand that, but I remember when my mom was really upset it would be me comforting her. When I was upset she would act like a spoiled brat and try and get attention. It seemed like I was always going to her, though, to help her out with her problems and to comfort her when she was feeling upset."

When role reversal occurs, responsibilities beyond the age and capacity of the child are often imposed on her. The child tends to develop a false sense of self and may, in turn, appear and act older than she is. As a result, she is expected to accept even greater responsibility. This process robs the child of her childhood.

The following excerpt explains the thoughts and feelings of a child who displays pseudomaturity. It is part of a letter written by Barbara, a twelve year old girl, who for most of her life cannot recall playing games and doing the things that young children normally do. For example, she does not remember playing with dolls or with other children her age, or riding bicycles. Barbara wrote this after disclosure, and about three months into treatment.

"The only thing I can say now is that I'm twelve years old again. I can laugh around with my friends or joke around and I don't have to pretend anymore that it's too immature. I realize that I've lived and experienced more things than probably my friends have, but that doesn't bother me anymore, because the thing that I'm allowed to do now is that I can let down my

---

Role Reversal

Parent
(mother)
↓
Seeks out person to meet emotional needs
↓
Is unable to find peer or spouse to meet these needs
↓
Seeks out child (usually child victim) to meet these needs
↓
Demands that child meet these needs
↓
Child accepts responsibility
↓
Role Reversal develops where the child parents the parent

Figure 3

Because these children have been forced to grow up so quickly,
and not allowed to develop emotions and behaviors appropriate to
childhood, they may struggle later, as adults, with the emergence
of infantile behavior. (See **Regressive or Infantile Behavior** on
page 25.)

Low Tolerance for Family Tension

Because many sexually abused children have been burdened
with the responsibility, or at least the feeling of responsibility for
the cohesiveness of their families, they are often afraid of tensions
being created in the family system.

If the father is the offender, he may have said to his child
(victim) that if the family breaks up, it is her fault. He may use
such manipulation to justify his sexual abuse of the child, telling
her that because his relationship with his wife (the child's
mother) is falling apart, it is the child's responsibility to keep
them together. He may also threaten the child with family
breakup if she discloses the sexual abuse.* As a result, a sexually
abused child often has low tolerance for tension within the family;
not only does she feel responsible for it, but often the offender
chooses times of high family tension to sexually assault her.
Frequently, in response to pressure from the offender, a child may
retract her disclosure of abuse in an attempt to "undo" the
tensions created as a result of bringing the abuse into the open.

In the example below, Tammy, a fourteen year old girl,
initially disclosed her abuse out of fear that Larry, her step-father,
was about to become physically abusive towards her mother. She
wrote the letter below just after she had retracted her statement to
authorities.

Dear Larry,
*I am so sorry that you are in trouble with the police for what I
did. I didn't mean to get you into trouble for this, I just wanted you*

* *Native children may also be subjected to pressure not to betray the family to
the white world or "alien outside others" who they believe are intent on
destroying Native families.*

to stop. I should have never led you to bed like I did, but I felt that you would not love mom or me if I did not do what you wanted in bed. I know that you are really tired when you get home from work and that you like to have your back rubbed down and I know that mom doesn't like to have sex with you as much as you want it. That's why I wanted to make you happy. But now you're in trouble for something I did. I'm really sorry for that. I will try and make things better for you when I talk to the police, and again soon we will be back home as a happy family. I'm so very sorry for hurting you.

   Love always,
   Tammy

This letter is very interesting in what it reveals about the dynamics of the relationship between the offender and his victim. In this case, Larry privately confronted Tammy after her disclosure and convinced her to retract her statement by promising not to hurt her mother. Larry built up Tammy's sense of guilt and responsibility for the turmoil that was created in the family due to the disclosure. Out of fear that the family would break up, and that she would be blamed for it, Tammy told the police and social workers that her initial allegations of abuse were fabricated. She wanted to return home and have a happy and stable family life.

She was eventually allowed to return home, but because her sexual abuse actually did occur, and the relationships with the family were dysfunctional, the family broke down quickly. Her mother and Larry separated and Tammy eventually went to a foster home. Larry was later charged with sexual abuse of a person under the age of 16.

Alienation from the Family

In any family in which incest is occurring on an ongoing basis, the relationships between all members of the family tend to be very unhealthy. The dysfunctional roles within the family can create opposing relationships and a sense of alienation of all family members from each other. This can be especially isolating for the child victim(s) in the family.

For example, Linda, a twelve year old child victim, was sexually assaulted by her father over a four year period. Although her mother had no direct knowledge that the sexual abuse was occurring, she did see "a special relationship" between her daughter and husband. She did not know how to deal with the relationship that she saw, but felt jealous and resentful. Linda also had a brother and sister, who as far as she was aware, were not being sexually assaulted by their father.

Over the years, Linda became very protective of her father even though he was sexually assaulting her. At the times when he touched her sexually, he would cry or express guilt and remorse for what he was doing. In the past he had told Linda that he was sorry for what he had done, but also said that the relationship between himself and Linda's mother was very hurtful for him.

Because Linda had a need to protect her father, she often became angry and resentful towards her mother for doing things that she thought hurt her father. At the same time, because Linda's mother resented the special relationship that she saw between her husband and daughter, she pulled away from and became angry towards Linda. She rationalized her withdrawal from her daughter and her outward expression of anger, because of how she felt about her relationship to the family. Thus mother and daughter became increasingly alienated from each other, each feeling powerful negative emotions towards the other.

A similar dynamic took place between Linda and her siblings. Her brother and sister also saw her relationship with her father as "special." For example, their father showed less anger towards Linda than other family members, and gave her certain gifts that he did not give to the other children. Naturally, when her siblings saw such favoritism, they became jealous and resentful and held back their affection from Linda; they came to treat her in the same hostile way as her mother.

The relationships that developed between all the members of the family were very unhealthy and dysfunctional. Each person felt alienated from the family as a whole, and that his/her needs were not being met. Victim, non-offending parent, siblings and offender, all feel, think, and behave in a similar manner towards others in the family.

Emotional Needs Towards the Father Offender

Amid the unhealthy relationships within the dysfunctional incestuous family, the sexually abused child may feel that the only person who shows her love and affection is the offender. When she was first touched, she may have been told that there was nothing wrong with the touching or she may have felt a sense of warmth, caring and love as a result of the encounter. The offender, as he was touching the child, probably told her that he loved her and that no one else made him feel the way she did. The victim may have felt special and cared for. As the other relationships in her life deteriorate, as she grows more distant from her mother, siblings, and possibly even her friends, she may crave for an acknowledgement of love and affection from her father, (the abuser). This does not mean that she wants to be sexually assaulted, but only that she is looking for confirmation that she is accepted, loved and needed. If the abuse occurs over a long period of time, the victim may develop a belief that sexual contact with the offender confirms that she is loved, cared for and accepted.

The following comments made by a victim in therapy illustrate these feelings:

"It seemed like my dad was the only person who paid attention to me. I realized that what he was doing to me was wrong but I knew that he was sick and needed help. I felt so protective of him that I was more willing to accept the pain than to hurt him. It seemed like I tried so hard for him to accept and love me that I was able to forgive him or deny what it was he was doing. It was easy to be angry at my mom, brothers and sisters because they never seemed to show any affection when my father did. I realized later that the affection my father showed me was really abuse in disguise."

Inability to Trust

Trust is a major issue for children who have been sexually assaulted. Since most victims are assaulted by people whom they have trusted, they believe that trusting has made them vulnerable. Consequently, they soon find it difficult to trust anyone including themselves.

Trusting is an issue for the child victim not only prior to and during the abuse, but also after disclosure when the abuse has ended. The severity of the child's inability to trust depends on a number of factors. For example, the relationship the child has had with the offender, the emotional psychological or physical pain she has endured, and the reaction she receives at the point of disclosure all affect her ability to trust others again. In some cases, the inability to trust others is also reflected in an inability to trust oneself as is reflected in the following excerpt:

"Even though trusting other people is a real big problem for me, I'm not sure if it's a bigger problem than the fact that I don't even trust myself. I don't think you can trust other people if you don't trust yourself. I know for me it's sure like that. Whenever I trusted anybody, including my family, they would always take advantage of me and hurt me. I don't think I'll ever let anybody do that again. But I know it's affecting me because I don't even trust myself enough to get out of the shell I am living in. I feel so insecure because of it and at times I wish it would just end."

Loneliness

Understandably, most incest and child sexual abuse victims express a deep sense of loneliness. They often say that they have been able to be with their friends or a crowd of people and still feel all alone. On the one hand, the child victim is often alienated from her family and finds no comfort there. And on the other, she may have been forced to limit her contacts with friends and others outside the family due to the offender's fear that she might reveal the sexual abuse. Victims are often warned not to talk with others about anything which happens in their families, or for that matter, about anything at all of a personal nature. As a result, the secrecy about family matters demanded by the offender carries over into other aspects of life. These children turn inward and learn to rely mostly on themselves. They become very guarded about their feelings, thoughts and actions and consequently, do not develop competent social skills or the skills of healthy self-expression.

"Most people think that the hardest thing for me was to keep the secret that my dad was touching me sexually. Yeah, sure, that was really hard, but some of the other things that were hard to keep were that I couldn't tell anybody that I was abusing drugs or alcohol, and that sometimes after certain things would happen to me I would cut myself up with a knife or a piece of glass. I also found it hard to keep secret the fact that I was seeing all sorts of my friends when my dad and mom said no I couldn't do it. Those things affected my life a lot. Sometimes I think even more so than the fact that I was keeping the secret that my dad touched me."

These children need to experience sharing not only their emotional pain, but happy and satisfying thoughts and experiences as well.

One victim expressed her loneliness and isolation this way:

"It seemed like I never felt happy anyway. No one would ever talk to me or share any of their feelings or thoughts. I always feel so all alone."

Depression

At one point or another, most if not all child sexual abuse victims are depressed. Many have unconsciously used depression as a method of coping, as it tends to block out any sense of feeling. Since feelings are a direct experience of oneself, the acknowledgement of feelings is a very painful process for these children; it brings back memories and experiences they would sooner forget.

In some cases victims are uncontrollably depressed; these children run a very high risk of committing suicide. (See **Suicide** on page 40.)

Anger and Aggression

Although many child sexual abuse victims appear passive and compliant on the outside, they may be seething with rage inside. They commonly develop a passive/aggressive attitude and when confronted, their anger can erupt explosively. A child victim may have learned that only through anger is she able to take a stand and voice her opinion. Or she may use anger as another method to disassociate herself from painful feelings she does not want to experience.

Consider the following case described by a victim in a treatment session:

"I realised the other night when I was going home that there was no way that I wanted to discuss with my parents what had happened to me. You see I was out and had sex with these two guys just after my father had sexually assaulted me. I hated the sex and I felt dirty and degraded during the act itself. On the way back home I was thinking a lot about it and I knew that I had a need to discuss it with somebody. I obviously couldn't discuss it with my dad because he was the one who had sexually assaulted me, and I thought I couldn't discuss it with my mom because she wouldn't understand.

I arrived home approximately 10 or 15 minutes prior to my curfew time. I knew that if I went into the house at this time my parents would be happy and would want to talk about the good things that happened to me when I was out for the night. I knew I couldn't deal with this so what I decided to do was to wait outside the house until it was approximately half an hour past my curfew time. I realized that when I went into the house a half an hour after, my parents would be very mad and angered with me and would send me straight to my room. I set that situation up specifically because I didn't know how to deal with the situation if my parents decided to actually talk to me.

When I opened the door and went into the house, the first thing that my Mom said to me was, 'Where the hell were you tonight, don't you know it's past your curfew time?' I could tell my dad felt a bit guilty because he had touched me sexually that night, that instead of bawling me out, he told my mom to shut up and leave me alone. The only thing that was done to me or asked of me was to send me to my room. The conversation between my mom and dad and I wasn't pleasant as I was yelling and swearing at them. However, inside of me I was saying I sure wish I could tell you what happened. However, once I went to my room I was able to fall asleep very quickly and drift off into a land where nobody could touch me at all. I spend a lot of time doing this, you know."

Phobias

Many sexually abused children suffer from fears or phobias as a result of the dynamics of the incestuous family or the sexual abuse itself. In some cases, the offender may deliberately create fears in the victim's mind in order to control her behavior, as in the following example:

"We lived in a neighbourhood where there were lots and lots of birds. After my father would touch me sexually he would tell me that he knew that I was thinking of telling somebody about the sexual abuse. He told me that whenever I would start to think that, birds would begin to fly overhead and at times some of them may hit the house. I realized I shouldn't have, but I did believe him that this was true. I found out later in treatment, from my father, that he said that specifically to keep me in line so I wouldn't tell anybody. The birds were always hitting the house and he used that method of controlling me."

In the case of this child, the phobia became so traumatic that she found it difficult to even pick up a paper or magazine that displayed pictures of birds. She carried this fear of birds with her into adulthood. As she got older, however, she discovered that when she told people she had a fear of birds, she received a lot of attention. Although it was for something that made her uncomfortable, she felt that the attention she got from this was worth the pain and suffering.

Along with her fear of birds, this person had many allergies. She explained that when she wasn't getting enough attention that her allergies would act up. She indicated that numerous times she would pretend that the problem was there to the point that she actually felt the symptoms. *(This is not to suggest that people who suffer from allergies create them themselves.)*

Often, a child who has been sexually abused by an adult, whether that adult be male or female, develops an acute fear of being in the presence of that adult. For example, when a four year old child, who was being sexually assaulted by her father, was picked up by her mother from the day care center, she met her with smiles and open arms. However, when the child's father picked her up, she expressed extreme anxiety and went with him very reluctantly, usually crying and often wetting or soiling her pants. In an interview she said:

"When Daddy was come to get me, I'm scared, he hurt me and made me bad....Mommy nicer and don't hurt me like Daddy. They should stop Daddy from taking me."

Later this child was able to say that she was angry not only at her father for doing what he did to her, but also at the staff of the daycare center "for allowing her father to do that." (In the mind of the child, the daycare staff were supporting what her father was doing to her.)

Even in older children, fear of the offender may be so extreme as to be experienced merely at the thought of being in his or her presence. Furthermore, the intensity of the fear can be as great for males who have been sexually assaulted by females, as for females who have been assaulted by males. Males develop a fear of females in respect to their dominance and control. Females can develop fears in respect to the male's physical power and control.

Here are two examples of these fears expressed by victims in therapy. The first is from a male victim of assault by females, the second from a female assaulted by a male.

"It might sound stupid to you but I couldn't tell anyone what my older sister and my aunt was doing to me. I thought first of all of telling somebody what they were doing to me but I knew that they would laugh at me and think that I was a suck if I was to tell them that it hurt what they were doing. So I kind of had to hide it. It seemed the more I hid it though, the more I really became afraid of women. I don't know, it seemed like somehow they had this control or power over me, and whenever I was around them I really started to shake and to sweat and it was really scary. I found that the only way I could really get rid of the scared feeling was to become really angry and threaten them. That seemed to work for the time being but even the more I did that the more I became afraid of them."

"Whenever I would even think about being around men, what I mean by this is, if I thought I would go to a store to buy something and the clerk at the store was a man or that I would have to stay in a room alone with a man, even if I knew him, I really got scared. I wasn't always afraid that he would sexually assault me but sometimes I was just afraid that maybe he would hurt me. It just seemed like I couldn't trust them."

In some cases, sexual assault victims develop a generalized fear of everything as in the following case.

"It seemed like I was afraid of everything, I couldn't go out of the house alone, especially if it was dark. It seemed like at one point in my life I couldn't even walk down the street if there were people there. I was just afraid of everything. I realize now that those fears that I had were unrealistic, but at the time I was living it, it felt like I was living in hell."

Sudden Changes in Behavior

The behavior patterns of sexually abused children can undergo sudden dramatic changes in response to a multitude of different situations. For example, a child may fear that the offender is about to sexually assault a sibling, and act out as a result. Behavior change can also occur during the transition from one form of sexually abusive behavior to another. The child may be very traumatized, for example, when the sexual abuse changes from fondling to intercourse, from fondling to oral sex, from masturbation to fondling, or in some other manner. Any of these traumas in the child's life can provoke behaviors which are uncharacteristic of her normal patterns.

Eating and Sleeping Problems

Many sexually abused children react to the stress levels within the family by either overeating or not eating enough. Some become anorectic or bulimic, and others, especially older children, purposely gain weight. Since victims often believe that the sexual abuse is being created in part by their looks, they may also believe that if they gain weight and become obese, that the offender(s) will not find them sexually attractive and the abuse will end. Of course, since incest and child sexual abuse is much more an exertion of power and domination over another than a matter of sexual attraction, the gained weight does not bring the abuse to an end, but instead serves to further damage the child's self image.

Abused children also often suffer from sleep disorders and/or sleep disturbances ranging from nightmares to excessive sleeping. (Of course, non-abused children sometimes experience these as well.) Many sexual abuse victims experience nightmares that are re-enactments of the sexual act, or of situations that create the same degree of fear. Through treatment these can be eliminated.

Other abused children use excessive sleeping as a means to escape the reality of their abuse. They believe that once they fall asleep they can free themselves of the pain they are experiencing. Usually during sleep they are able to fantasize and dream of situations other than what is occurring in their lives. Many of these children sleep 12 to 15 hours per day, or even more.

For example, Linda, thirteen, and her brother Kevin, fifteen, were both sexually assaulted by different members of their immediate and extended family. The sexual abuse involved intercourse ynd fondling and occurred over a period of five years.

Both children found it difficult to cope with the abuse and reacted in a similar manner. Linda spent most of her time in her bedroom either studying for school or sleeping. She would spend approximately 12 - 15 hours per day sleeping, and on weekends she usually slept well into the afternoon. She got up for a few hours to eat, and then went back to bed. Her mom was concerned that Linda was not associating with friends, but because she got good marks in school, didn't comment on how much Linda slept.

Similarily, Kevin spent most of his time, including weekends, sleeping; his waking hours were usually between 11:00 p.m. and 3:00 or 4:00 a.m. His parents would ridicule him for being lazy. Kevin said that he used to find it difficult to concentrate and pay attention in school. As a result, he got expelled just before his fifteenth birthday.

In treatment, Kevin and Linda explained why they spent so much time in their rooms. They said that sleeping allowed them an opportunity to "drift off into a fantasy land" and escape the reality of their abuse.

Regressive or Infantile Behavior

Sometimes children who have lost their childhood through role reversal and pseudomaturity, will display regressive or "infantile" behavior at an older age. This behavior is painful for victims because it reflects a sense of loss, and brings back memories they would sooner forget. At the same time, however, it serves as a method of coping with stress and uncomfortable situations.

"Sometimes when I was depressed I can remember curling up in a little ball in my bed and rocking back and forth. I felt better being surrounded by my stuffed animals because they seemed to be my only friend. Even in writing this it's sad to think that at twenty-six years old I still have to do that."

Extreme Behavior Related to Personal Hygiene

Sexually abused children display a wide range of behaviors related to their own personal hygiene and grooming. Often, children who inwardly feel terrible about themselves as a result of their victimization, display their feelings through their personal appearance. One victim expressed it this way:

"I felt so terrible inside I just couldn't get myself together to take a shower, or even wash my hair. I realized that I was starting to stink. But I accepted it fully because it reflected how I felt anyways."

Sometimes, children will behave in just the opposite manner, by displaying a false sense of self through meticulous grooming habits. Another victim described her behavior as follows:

"The only way I could escape reality was to pretend that things were going o.k. The only way I knew best to do this was to make myself look beautiful. I usually spent hours in front of the mirror before I would go to school, and people would always comment on how nice I looked. This made me feel real good, and I convinced myself that people would only make nice comments to people who were actually really nice and had no problems."

Behavior which may seem related to hygiene, but is undertaken for different reasons, is the taking of excessive numbers of baths or showers.

In this case, the behavior is provoked not by a need to present good grooming, but by a desire to wash away the pain of the sexual abuse. Often after the sexual abuse, especially if intercourse has occurred, the child will take a bath or shower in an attempt to rid herself of the reality of what has occurred. Victims may feel so dirty thinking about it that they will take two or three baths during a given day.

Some girls have taken scrub brushes to their vaginal area and scrubbed to the point of bleeding in a desire to feel clean again. One victim described her behavior this way:

"I just couldn't do anything until I took a bath and scrubbed off the filth and the scum that he put there. Sometimes I would scrub so hard, well, the area between my legs became really tender. Sometimes it would actually bleed because I scrubbed so hard. I would never tell anybody about the fact that I was scrubbing so hard down there, except one time when I was a little girl my mom found out that I was doing that and took me to the doctor. That was the most horrible time in my life, to have a doctor look at me down there. I swore I would never go to a doctor again. To this day I haven't. If anybody even suggests that I have a problem there, I deny it, because there is no way that I will ever allow that to happen again."

Related to the feeling of being "unclean" is a strong fear that nudity exposes the sexual abuse to others. For this reason, many child sexual abuse victims find it extremely uncomfortable to undress in front of peers.

For example, this can cause acute anxiety for girls who are required to shower after physical education classes in school. (See **School Related Problems** on page 31.)

Excessive Concern About Night-time Security

Many sexually abused children who are unwilling to disclose their abuse out of fear that they will not be believed, feel that securing their bedrooms is their only alternative. Such a child will often go to the extreme of putting a lock on the door which can be opened only from the inside, or of barricading the door by moving a dresser or desk up against it so that the offender cannot enter.

"Well, I couldn't tell anybody. The only way I could stop it was to lock my door so he couldn't enter it. Usually he would only touch me in my room. So I thought if I blocked the door he wouldn't touch me. When I think about it now it's funny that my mom never questioned me why I would always put my dresser and things in front of my door at night. I'm still not sure why she accepted the stupid excuse that I was afraid that burglars would come in."

If the child suspects that her siblings are also targets of the offender, she may try to ensure their safety by bringing them into her bedroom, especially if she feels that her effort to protect herself puts them at greater risk.

Frequently, the offender has convinced the child that she is able to protect her siblings by allowing her abuse to continue. As a result, if the child tries to end the abuse by locking or barricading her door, she will often want to extend the same night time protection to her siblings by physically moving them into her bedroom.

"There's no way I was going to allow him to touch them too. I even told him once straight to his face that if he ever touched them I was going to tell somebody what he was doing. You should have seen the look on his face when I said that. I didn't think that that scare alone was going to stop him, so I took over the responsibility of looking after my sister and brother. Even to the point of where I took them in my room and let them sleep there. I knew then that if my dad came in I would at least hear him and I could stop him."

If the child who is concerned about the security of her siblings feels helpless to protect them, she may try to insulate herself from this emotional pain through withdrawal, creating emotional distance from her siblings. She feels that if she is emotionally detached, the pain of helplessness will be easier to deal with. (See **Withdrawal** on the next page.)

Withdrawal

Withdrawal, in different forms, is very widely used by sexually abused children. Many of them have realized that voicing their opinion and taking a stand gets them nowhere. Instead, they become skilled at withdrawing, a defense mechanism which allows them to escape from the reality of what is occurring.

"It wasn't wise in our family to say anything to anybody. If you did it seemed like you either got smacked or sexually abused. I soon realized that if I shut up and kind of just pulled inward and didn't really focus on anything, that people would leave me alone."

Through withdrawal, sexually abused children escape into a world where it is usually difficult to reach them, giving them a sense of some control and direct power over themselves. They may attempt this escape through alcohol and/or drug abuse, or prostitution.

Alcohol and/or Drug Abuse

When sexually abused children are unable to escape from the reality of their lives through simple withdrawal and through fantasy, they may try to blot out the pain of their existence with alcohol and/or drugs. These provide additional means with which to numb the feelings associated with their abuse.

"By getting drunk and stoned all the time it seemed like I ran further and further away from the problem. The more stoned and drunk I got the less I felt. It didn't work, however, because it finally caught up with me."

Many sexually abused children have developed alcohol and/or drug dependencies which must be dealt with in addition to the problems related to the sexual abuse. A Native girl describes the cycle of alcoholism and sexual abuse in her own life this way:

"My name is Coline and I was sexually assaulted by my dad and two of his brothers. Also my brothers sexually abused me. I am sixteen years old now, and I've been sexually abused for seven and a half years, that I can remember. Everybody where I lived were always drunk and everybody was being sexually abused. I couldn't tell anybody about it because I was scared that I would be hurt. Before I was sexually abused I was drinking only a little bit but after I was sexualy abused I became an alcoholic. Everybody else that I saw was an alcoholic 'cause alcohol kills the pain. My pain was from sexual abuse and the alcohol I drank killed it.

After we left the reserve I met lots of people who didn't drink but I kept drinking because the sexual abuse kept going on. It seemed like whenever I was sexually abused or started thinking about the sexual abuse I would have to go out and get drunk. Usually when I went out and got drunk I also usually got raped."

A rising concern in some Native communities is the use of inhalents by many young people. These children may be "sniffing" or "huffing" to help kill the pain of sexual abuse.

Sexual Promiscuity

Substance abuse is sometimes associated with sexual promiscuity. Sexually abused children may have learned at a young age that sexuality or sexual intercourse, is connected to feelings of being loved and cared for. At times, however, they may also believe that the sexual acts themselves are quite abusive. As a result of these conflicting beliefs, many sexual abuse victims display promiscuous behavior. Nonetheless, they usually experience much more pain, distance, and sense of numbing than pleasure during the sexual act, and their bad feelings about their own behavior may give them further cause to kill the pain with drug or alcohol abuse as is described below by one victim:

"When I was out during the evening, I couldn't stop thinking about the fact that my father had intercourse with me tonight. The more I thought about that the more lonely and distant I got from any sense of being loved or cared for. Once I got to the party I looked for a guy that I was somewhat attracted to but didn't really know very well. I immediately came on to him, in hopes that he would have intercourse with me that night. As it turned out he did as well as another guy did. During the sexual acts I initially felt a sense of love and caring, and tried to convince myself that they did it because they loved me. However, as it continued I became more repulsed and felt degraded and dirty. After I had sex twice, I didn't know how to deal with that and also what my dad did, so I dealt with it in the only way I knew best, and that was to get drunk and stoned. At least when I'm drunk and stoned I have the ability to convince myself that none of the other things happened at all. I usually try to go to bed stoned or drunk, because then I can get into a quick sleep. When I wake up in the morning I can convince myself that it was all a dream."

Withdrawal from Friendships

The sexually abused child is often forced by the incest offender to withdraw from peer relationships. When the father offender feels threatened by his victim's social contacts outside the home, he may demand that they be discontinued. If the victim complies, she loses a needed support system.

"It seemed like my dad was so afraid that the secret of what he was doing to me would get out that he made it that my mom couldn't go anywhere. My brother and sister couldn't have any friends over and neither could I. I don't know whether or not my brother and sister saw their friends. I know that I did, which even made it harder. I remember once I brought my friends home from school when I thought my dad wasn't there. He was really mad when he found my friends and I in my room. At first when he saw them there he treated them real nice and asked them if they wanted anything to eat or to drink. But then after they left he got so angry at me and yelled at me and told me that if I ever did that again, I would be in lots of trouble. My friends always liked him so it made it even more difficult when I had to pretend for some other reason why they couldn't come over to my house anymore."

Running Away

When keeping a low profile, fantasy, withdrawal and chemical escape cease to be an effective means of coping with abuse, children will often physically leave the abusive environment; they run away.

Usually, the children who run away believe that they have asked for assistance either directly or indirectly and felt that they were denied or shunned.

"It seemed like I told everybody about what was happening but nobody would listen. They finally listened when I packed my bags and left."

Inappropriate Peer Relationships

Because many children who are sexually assaulted develop pseudomaturity at an early age, they often tend to seek out and associate with older people. Role reversal in their incestuous families has deprived them of childhood, and they have had to bypass or ignore much of their own emotional and psychosocial development. In adulthood, many of these people seek out a partner considerably older than themselves. The sexual assault victim is able to ignore a very large age gap between herself and her partner as is revealed in the following case.

"I sure got a lot of flack from my friends and family because this guy I was falling in love with was really old enough to be my father. But you know he seemed so warm and caring and he made me feel so secure. I realize that he was 34 years older than me but I didn't think that he was too much like my dad. At least not then. When I look back at it though, my dad was pretty demanding and so was Bill. My dad really liked to control my life and actually so does Bill. My dad used to abuse me sexually. I don't think Bill abuses me sexually but sometimes I know he makes me have sex with him when I don't want it. Maybe Bill's a lot more like my dad than I realize."

Lying

Instances of children making false accusations of sexual abuse in order to get back at a parent are extremely rare. Children are much more likely to distort the truth in order to conceal abuse, particularly intercourse if it has occurred than to fabricate abuse. One child expressed the pain of telling the truth this way:

"I wish I was lying because it would be easier to deal with a lie than with the truth, because you see the truth really hurts."

Lying on the part of sexual abuse victims must be looked at in context. On the one hand, the child is actively encouraged by the offender to lie to others about the relationships within the incestuous family, and on the other, she is penalized if she makes false statements about other issues.

"I told you the truth most of the time, but after a while I knew that you wouldn't believe me so I said whatever came to my mind. I had to lie about what you were doing to me so I may as well lie about everything else in my life."

Further confusion is created in the child's mind because she believes that she has told the truth about certain situations over and over again and we, as adults, have missed it or accused her of lying. This leads the child to believe that telling the truth is not worthwhile because she doesn't get the desired response of trust, support and acceptance.

School Related Problems

Many children who have been traumatized through physical, emotional or sexual abuse will perform poorly in school or display behavior problems. Others, through single-minded commitment to academic pursuits, will use school as an outlet in order to escape the reality of their home situations.

"I didn't know what to do to get my mind off what my father was doing to me. The only thing I could come up with was to drown myself in school work."

"The only way that I could prove that I was something was to get good grades, everything at home was falling apart, and I wasn't able to spend much time with my friends any more. It seemed that everything was falling apart. I think that the only way that I was to survive this was to work really hard at school. When I would achieve things there, it would make me feel like I accomplished something and that I was worth something."

Other children, unfortunately, experience severe problems in school that are related to the abusive home situation. These can range from lack of motivation, to outright hostility.

"It seemed that every time I tried to do something everybody would say that I was a failure. Pretty soon after hearing it so much I really believed that I was. I knew that I could do better at home and do better in school, but it seemed like everybody expected me to fail, and so I did. I didn't really want to skip school but sometimes I got accused of doing so when I didn't. I became so frustrated with being accused of doing things I didn't do, that I decided it was a losing battle and I did it anyways. I know I could have done better in school, but it seemed like such a waste of time when nobody else cared."

Although the inappropriate behaviors that children exhibit in school are a sign of distress and often a cry for help, because they cause problems for teachers and the institution, they are often met with punishment and rejection.

Poor Attention Span

Many children who have been sexually abused find it difficult to concentrate on a given topic for any length of time. This may result from behavior learned to help cope with the abuse. The child may believe that if she concentrates too much on a particular topic that she will be unable to distract her mind from thinking about the abuse she is subjected to.

Another cause of poor attention span could be that the victim's mind is constantly bombarded with conflicting thoughts and feelings, thus preventing her from maintaining concentration. Of course, this causes problems for students in school, as a child victim describes on the following page:

"I just couldn't seem to concentrate on anything. My mind would always wander and if I stopped to think of anything for too long the thoughts about my dad always came back. The teachers at school used to get really mad at me for that, because they always said I wasn't paying attention to them. I think if they knew why I wasn't paying attention to them maybe they wouldn't have gotten so mad."

Truancy

There may be a number of different reasons why sexually abused children avoid school. In some cases children believe that they are forced to live a lie at school because they must conceal the abuse they are experiencing and pretend that everything is alright.

Sometimes children are afraid that other children at school might be able to see that they have been sexually abused simply by looking at them. In order to avoid showering in front of other girls, female victims may skip school or engage in hostile behavior. Truancy can be a symbolic cry for help from a sexually abused child. Unfortunately, it is often rewarded with expulsion from school, reinforcing the child's sense of worthlessness and view of the world as unjust.

Hostile Behavior

As with truancy, hostile behavior towards teachers and the school in general can have several different causes. In some cases, it is a deliberate strategy to provoke expulsion. This may be desired, for example, in order to end the lie that victims believe they are living at school. One victim described her plan this way:

"I was just fed up with going to school and having to pretend like everything at home was alright. I just couldn't take it anymore, so I kept on blowing up at the teacher in hopes that they would finally kick me out. I knew that the school was pretty strict on mouthing off teachers so that's what I did. As a result I got expelled from school. When I got expelled I at least didn't have to face the people at school and pretend any more."

Another girl created problems at school in order to avoid physical education classes which required undressing and showering in front of others.

"When I signed up for school this term, I did whatever I could to avoid taking my physical education class. Unfortunately, the counsellor said that the school had some policy that everybody was required to do it in the grade I was in. When I first heard that, I

thought of withdrawing from school completely, because the thought of going to that class terrified me. However, I was talked in to enrolling anyways. The first few times that I went to class I took hold of any excuse that I could grab on to, so that I didn't have to change in front of other people. I told the teacher that I forgot my gym strip at home, somebody stole my gym strip, I had a rash all over my body and any other thing I could think of. After a while the excuses didn't work, so what I had to do was create a problem before going to gym class so that I was sent down to the office. Usually what I would do was start a fight or an argument with the teacher in the class before gym class. My punishment usually was to have to go to the office and wait to speak to the principal. That usually meant that I had to sit there through the whole other class. I did this a few times to the point of being expelled from school and then I made a deal with the teacher that what I would do was instead of wearing shorts and taking a shower, I enrolled in an activity that made it that I had to leave school right after gym class. So what I did was to wear a sweat suit to gym class and then leave class right after. In doing this I avoided having to take a shower or being seen in shorts or cut offs."

The Secret Loser

*Doesn't she look great, so confident. She is such a perfectionist,
always trying to do better. She really has her head on straight.
She sure knows where she is going, the model human being.
Everyone's ideal person; so cheery, friendly and open to all.
She's so willing to help anybody. I bet she has a lot of friends
and a very comfortable homelife.
But what of her homelife? If only they knew. I'm the perfect pretender.
I have problems just like everyone else.
Would people like me as much if they knew what I was really like?
And what friends? I don't have any really close friends, sincere friends.
What does a sincere friend look like?
Would I recognize one if one were standing in front of me.
My homelife is non existent. When I am there, it is my physical being only.
I am a prisoner of myself, held captive by my emotions,
not willing to show people who I really am.
Work is a refuge for me.
Isn't it funny how a person can be almost robotic in their work place?!
That's me, the robot. If you look close enough, you might even see my program.
I am scared of everything; changes, new ideas, how people will think of me, etc...
I am what you might call a secret loser.
I mean, look at what I'm losing out on; friends, family, fun, excitement...,life.
I am great at pretending. Not unlike a robot, I don't show pain, hurt, tears.
I never said I didn't feel those emotions, just never showed them.
I bet you didn't even know.
I hid them well...
I hid me!*

Nadine Callihoo Oshanyk
November 11, 1987

Inappropriate Sexual Knowledge and/or Play

Knowledge of Sexual Matters

Many young child sexual abuse victims express knowledge of sexual matters which is far from age appropriate. Children expressing such knowledge have been taught it, seen it, or experienced it. Usually, sexual encounters experienced by children have provided them with models of behavior which are abusive and damaging to them. Later, such knowledge impairs their ability to develop healthy relationships which involve intimacy and/or sexuality as adults.

For a number of reasons, many child sexual abuse victims provide hints about their sexual activity. Sometimes victims view themselves as promiscuous and/or "dirty", possibly as a result of being told this by their peers or significant others such as family members. If this has occurred, hinting about such activity reinforces their negative self image and self worth, which in turn, allows them to justify the way they feel and behave.

Hinting about sexual activity is also a cry for help, a message that things are not okay, which the victim hopes others will pick up and respond to.

"It seemed like whenever I got into trouble I would throw out some stupid comment like 'I guess you think I was sleeping around, don't you', or 'I bet you think I'm a slut, don't you.' I wasn't really doing all those things but I thought if I said that maybe my mom would look into what I was saying and find out that my dad was sexually assaulting me. It seemed, though the more hints I would give her about what was going on, the further away she looked.

I even went as far as leaving letters and poems lying around the house, that had a lot of sexual information in it. Once I even remember putting my diary out on the kitchen table so that my mom would find it. She read the diary where I had talked about being sexually active and doing all sorts of stuff like that and even she read the part where I told the diary that I didn't like what my dad was doing to me. I realize I didn't spell it right out and say that dad was touching me sexually, but I did hint to it. When my mom read this it didn't seem to click in with her, 'cause all she did was get angry at me for being a slut. It seemed like nothing I did got through to her that I needed help."

Literature and Art With Sexual Themes

Often children will express emotional, psychological, physical or sexual abuse in their poems and literature or art work. In some cases, the sexual content of their drawings is explicit and easily seen. In others, the clues to sexual abuse lie beneath the surface and require some probing to be understood. The tracing shown on the opposite page (the original picture was drawn with pencil crayons) represents an example of this.

It was made by a 6 year old girl when asked to draw a picture of her family and herself in a manner which explained their relationship. She was given no direction other than this.

When I initially spoke to the child about her drawing, she indicated that it was a picture of her family standing in the doorway, and that she was outside playing. She said that the sun in the top left corner represented "Billy" (not his real name), a ten year old boy who attended her school and whom she liked very much. She provided me with very little other information, and no indication that any form of sexual abuse had occurred.

Because people's pictures of the sun are often symbolic of something that is warm, comforting and trusting, I decided to talk to Billy to see if he knew anything about this child's background. He gave me a long detailed account of sexual abuse that his friend, the child victim, had described.

After talking to Billy, I went back and spoke with the young girl who then explained her picture. The house represented to her, a place where the four members of her family would live, but where she didn't belong. She said that her father would come into her bedroom and "touch her private parts" at night and that, initially, she would just pretend to be asleep.

She went on to say that the more he continued to touch her, the harder it was for her to deal with it in this manner. She further explained that she then would "withdraw" herself from her body and pretend to stand beside the bed looking at the child (herself) lying on the bed being touched by her father. This method of dealing with the problem also became ineffective as time progressed.

Later the child would withdraw from her body and pretend to float around the room as she was being assaulted. After her father left the room, initially, she would come right back into her body. However, even that became difficult, and at times, she would "stay up there" for hours.

As the nature of the abuse became more traumatic for the child, her ability to cope with it by staying in the same room became more difficult. She said that she later would withdraw herself and would float among the clouds in the sky when her father was there. Instead of peering down at the child, many times she would just pretend that she was a bird floating among the clouds and trees. After her father had left the room, she would later re-enter her body.

I asked the little girl what would she have done if the abuse became worse. Where would she go, for example, if she could no

Facsimile of a drawing by a 6 year old child victim of incest

longer stay in the sky? Quite emphatically the child said: "I would then have to die."

In 6 short years, this girl had gone from living the life of a child, playing children's games, to learning how to defend herself from abuse and, eventually, death. (This child is now 18 years old and is working on a university business degree.)

Inappropriate Sexual Play

Some younger children who have a history of sexual abuse will be involved in sexual play with their peers/age mates, or with younger or older children. Quite often these children believe that touching in this manner indicates a sense of love, security, and overall well being.

Younger children often reinact with other children, the sexual exploitation that they have experienced. For example they may fondle other children or attempt intercourse or oral sex.

Diane, for example, is a six year old girl who was sexually assaulted by her father for approximately two years. The sexual abuse included the viewing of pornographic materials as well as oral and anal sex. When Diane found herself in a stressful situation at school she would complain of headaches and stomach aches, both symptoms she felt when she was being sexually assaulted. Diane later explained that in order to alleviate these pains she needed to play out her father's sexual molestation. Diane would encourage young children during recess, lunch or after school to pull down their pants and then engage in oral sex and anal penetration with their fingers or other objects. Diane said that during these times her stomach ache and headache would go away.

In another case, Ken, an eight year old boy, was sexually assaulted by his aunt and female babysitter on several occasions over a period of a year and a half. The last incident occurred when he was seven years old. During Ken's sexual exploitation by his aunt he was dressed up in adult clothes and told to pretend that he was grown up. Ken then was made to pretend as if he was forcing his aunt into sexual activity. The aunt would scream and yell and ask him not to touch her. Ken soon began to relate to most females in a similar manner and believed that that was the way they wanted to be treated. The babysitter who had sexually assaulted Ken explained in an interview that "Ken seemed so grown up and domineering that it was almost like he was a real man. I'm not sure why but I was attracted to that and I got him to have sex with me." Ken's situation was discovered when he would have younger girls at his school perform the same acts which he had been taught to commit.

It is important to note that not all sexual play is an indication of sexual abuse. Many children will explore their sexuality by touching themselves or other children out of natural curiosity. The issue is not the touching, but why it is occurring. A large age difference between the children involved in sexual play with each other (for example a ten year old touching a two year old) is a concern.

Sexual Abuse of Others

Many child sexual abuse victims have sexually assaulted children they have babysat. If this touching has occurred prior to the child disclosing her own sexual abuse (which is often the case), she may deny the abuse she has suffered, in order to conceal the abuse she has committed.

"When I first began babysitting I looked forward to the opportunity to look after some other children. I wanted to do for these children some of the things that I never had when I was younger. What I mean by this is, to give them love and caring, like I never had. I remember once when I was looking after this young boy and his sister, I got them both to take a bath together, so that I could put them to bed. When I had them in the bath and was washing them, for some reason I became drawn to touching his penis and her vagina. When I was doing this, I said over and over in my mind that this can't be happening and I've got to stop. But for some reason I wasn't able to stop. When I was touching them I decided that I would take my own clothes off and climb into the bathtub with them. When I was in the bathtub with them I got them to start playing with my breasts and my vagina, and I tried to have the boy have intercourse with me. When the social worker came to ask me about whether or not my father ever sexually assaulted me, the first thing that came back to my mind was what I did to this boy and girl. I thought to myself that if I told the social worker that my dad did this, that I would also have to tell her what I did to those kids. In order for me to avoid telling her what I did to the kids, I told her that my father never touched me at all."

Although this girl experienced the pain and traumatization of being sexually abused herself, this did not deter her from sexually abusing others. Younger children may encourage this form of sexual contact for reasons other than normal sexual exploration and this must be addressed appropriately.

Sadistic or Self-abusive Behavior

Some child sexual abuse victims develop sadistic behavior primarily towards animals or other children. Many of them experience power over others and use this to maintain some sense of self. Unfortunately, this process is damaging to other people and animals, sometimes to the point of causing death. Consider the following examples:

"I realized I didn't have control over my life until I discovered the feeling I got when I tortured animals. Even though I felt very bad doing what I did, I nonetheless felt powerful in controlling over something."

"I never really wanted to hurt them, I just found that after I started pushing them around I couldn't stop anymore. I realized that if I told them that I would beat them up again and hurt them even more if they told anybody what I did to them, that this gave me somewhat of a good feeling. Unfortunately, it got out of control, and I actually began torturing them. And I just seemed like I couldn't stop."

Often I have heard the word "masochistic behavior" being interchanged with sadistic behavior. I think it should be clarified that sadistic behavior is quite different from masochistic behavior. Sadists derive pleasure from inflicting pain on another. Masochists receive pleasure from being hurt or humiliated. I question whether or not the child victim who is perceived as being a sadist receives pleasure from hurting animals, or whether this behavior reinforces a negative self-concept and actually induces more pain than pleasure.

Similarly, I question whether or not "masochistic" child sexual abuse victims receive pleasure from inflicting pain upon themselves. Usually the process of self inflicting pain is and/or should be referred to as "self abusive behavior" as opposed to masochism. Self-inflicted pain is usually a reinforcement of the image of self and is used more as punishment than as a source of pleasure.

Suicide

It's unclear how many child sexual abuse victims commit suicide. Although many of them leave letters behind, they don't always describe the sexual abuse that has occurred in their lives.

At times, however, they do leave letters that describe the pain and torment that life has brought them. Consider the following examples:

Dear Brian,
I know that when you read this letter you will probably have already heard the news. I know that you tried to help me. But I think that the help came a little too late for me. I already feel at

peace with my life and I hope that you will understand that I had to do what I thought was best. As you know I did. If I could tell you just how I feel inside then maybe I would also have to tell myself that it was true, and I just can't do that. Maybe if I didn't take matters as far then I could have, but I don't really know. I guess we will never know. I hope that you really know that I am sorry for the problems that I have caused for you and for everyone. And I hope that some day you will all forgive me for this, but please don't forget me. I feel that I wasn't meant to be here and that's why I did this. If only there could have been another way, but I guess that this was meant to be. Goodbye for now.
Love,
Kathy.

Dear Alex,
I hope you will not be too mad at me for not coming to see you anymore. I feel that I am going through this alone and I don't think that I have the strength to fight on. I know that you are doing what you can and that you want to help me, but please don't waste your time. Please help someone else who is worthy of you and wants your help. Mom still doesn't believe me and I think that the police think that I am lying about what I am saying. I wish that I were lying about this but I am not. If they could feel the pain that I feel right now maybe they would charge him. Mom says that because the police aren't charging him it means that he didn't do it. She says that the law knows these things. When I spoke with the police officer he asked me a lot of questions. I didn't want to tell him everything because I was afraid of what he would think of me. I think that he understood what I was saying because he said that he knew it was hard for me to talk to him. I liked him. But why didn't he charge dad for what he did to me? You helped me a lot, Alex, and I will never forget you for what you did for me. I know that you will be worried when you find this letter, but I want you to know that I will be O.K. Thanks again for your help.
Your friend forever,
Chris

Both Chris and Kathy successfully committed suicide, one by an overdose of drugs and the other by taking drugs and drowning. In looking back on their lives, people were able to discover a multitude of ways that these two children were telling people that they weren't doing very well and that they needed help. Unfortunately, in their situations, help did not arrive.

Chapter 4
Characteristics of An Incest Offender

Introduction

As with the victims of incest or child sexual abuse, there is no single profile of the perpetrators of abuse. (See *offender,* and *incest offender* in the Glossary for definitions.) There are, however, a number of pronounced characteristics that are often exhibited by offenders. Perhaps the most surprising feature of these characteristics, is their unexceptional nature; they are common among members of society as a whole.

It is, therefore, virtually impossible to point out offenders from others in a crowd, as they blend in quite effectively. They often function well at their jobs, feeling less threatened there than at home.

Readers who are familiar with the profiles of alcoholics and spousal abusers will find that their upbringing and lifestyles, coping strategies, rationalizations and defense mechanisms are similar to those of incest offenders.

Bearing in mind the profile of the victim of incest or child sexual abuse, readers will also see similarities between the characteristics of victims and offenders. The reasons for this should become clear as we examine the offender's family history.

Family History of Offenders

Abusive Background

Most incest offenders have been sexually abused as children and have felt the pain, anguish and torment of being a victim. They have carried these feelings into adulthood and deal with them in a manner which contributes to the dysfunction of their families.

"For the life of me I can't understand why I would touch my child in a sexual way because that's exactly what happened to me when I was a kid. I was touched by my father, my aunt and my older sister and I think I was touched by one or two babysitters, I can't remember. I know what it feels like to be hurt and to have to live with being sexually abused. So I don't really understand why I would have touched my child, knowing how much it hurt."

Many other offenders who were not themselves sexually assaulted, experienced sexual abuse indirectly when they were children.

"I don't recall being sexually assaulted myself, but I knew that my father was sexually assaulting my sister, 'cause on a couple of times I caught him. First time actually my sister came and told me, but I didn't believe it. I didn't believe that my father could do something like that. But then a couple of times I caught him doing it. Once was in his bedroom when my mom was in the hospital and the other time was out in the barn. I think that just even knowing that hurt me a lot and I didn't know how to deal with that. My sister wanted me to tell somebody about it, but I didn't know what to do."

In other cases, the abuse experienced by the offender was not sexual; it could have been physical, or emotional. However virtually all incest offenders have, as children, experienced one or more forms of abuse.

Rigid Moralistic, Religious Upbringing

Many offenders come from very rigid moralistic and religious backgrounds.

"I came from a background where my mom and dad were really religious. It seemed like my dad lived by the letter of the Bible. If we disobeyed in any way whatsoever, we sure knew it, 'cause we really got it from him."

Often the offender learns as he is growing up, that the Bible (or other spiritual beliefs*) can be misused to justify the role of father as the head of the household who can demand and receive obedience from his wife and children. He carries this learning over into his own parenting as an adult. (See **Rigid Moralistic Parenting Style** on page 53.)

Stereotyped Sex Roles

Most incest offenders have learned a rigid, traditional sense of their own manhood, and stereotyped attitudes about sex roles for men and women. They have developed this "macho" sense of

---

**Some Native offenders have also hidden behind traditional Native spirituality. Often people are afraid to question someone whose stance seems to come from values and beliefs that they themselves cherish. It's as if we confuse the person with the beliefs. Many offenders understand this fear and use it to their advantage. They manipulate concepts as well as human beings.*

manhood from stereotypes in the media, from the role models provided by their fathers and from the relationship between their fathers and mothers.*

"My father said to me when I was really young that men don't cry. I kept on repeating that over and over in my head. 'Men don't cry. Men don't cry.' So when I got older and felt pain I realized that I could never cry. My mom died when I was really young and I remember feeling a lot of pain when she died. But I kept saying to myself, 'Men don't cry.' For a while I wondered whether I was gay because even though I was saying in my head, 'Men don't cry', I was also saying to myself, 'I sure feel like crying.' My dad always said that women cry because women were sissys. I began to see myself like a sissy because I knew that I wanted to cry but there was no way that I could show it."

Not surprisingly, most male offenders have experienced severe relationship problems with their own fathers. Typically, the offender's father has usually spent little time developing a healthy relationship with his son. In addition, he has not been a good role model for healthy male behavior. Through his own rigid, stereotyped attitudes, he has usually modeled an inability to express love, caring, concern and support.

"All I wanted from my dad was for him to show that he cared for me. I can't remember the last time he ever said I love you. I definitely can't remember the last time he gave me a hug or something like that. He thinks it's kind of strange and weird for a man to give another man a hug. But you know, down deep in my heart I really wanted that. I think my life would have been very different if I knew my dad loved me and he spent time with me. I swore when I was a teenager that if I had children that I would never ever do that to them and I would spend all this time with them and make them feel loved and cared for. After I started having children, I didn't know how to spend time with them. I didn't know how to say I loved them. I think I got that from my family. I'm not trying to blame them when I say that, it's just that I don't know how anybody can show love or caring for somebody else if they've never been taught how to."

Many Experiences of Failure While Growing Up

Many offenders come from backgrounds of emotional deprivation which have developed into a strong sense of insecurity. They have often had a succession of experiences which

Native offenders may have learned these roles in an institutional setting such as a residential school.

---

reinforce their view of themselves as failures.

"It seemed like my whole life was made up of everything going wrong. Looking back now, I don't think I know how to get out of any situation or to deal with anything in a proper way."

Many experiences of failure are related to the offender's inability to develop meaningful interpersonal relationships.

"I didn't really have too many girl friends, 'cause most of the relationships I had ended pretty badly. Most of the girls at school didn't pay too much attention to me anyways, and if one did, it seemed like the only reason they did was because they felt sorry for me and it really wasn't because they liked me."

Successive failures during childhood and adolescence in establishing satisfactory peer relationships, reinforces the future offender's negative self image, which he carries through to adulthood. In some cases, the failure comes about as a result of his own fear of personal involvement, and his tendency to flee or destroy a relationship at times of intimacy and/or commitment as in the following two cases:

"Even though I spent most of my life living on a farm, thinking back I don't think that was the reason I spent so much time by myself. I didn't know how to develop a relationship with anybody and whenever I started getting close it became quite scary and I had to end it because I didn't know how to continue it."

"Ya, I had lots of girlfriends, but whenever they started getting serious with me I had to break it off. I wasn't sure what they wanted or why they wanted to get serious. All I know is that it really bothered me and so I ended it."

Psychological Characteristics

Because of his series of failed relationships and the other unresolved issues of his past, the incest offender tends to lack any sense of comfort, direction, security and happiness in life. Although he may feel sorry for himself, he doesn't connect with or understand others' feelings (lacks empathy).

Low Self-Esteem

Like the victim, the incest offender generally holds himself in very low regard. This results from his own experience of abuse, his feelings of being unloved in his family of origin, and his alienation from his own father. His history of failures in establishing satisfying interpersonal relationships and the feelings of inadequacy which they have produced, also contribute towards his negative self image and low self-esteem.

Generally, incest offenders lack an assertive, self-actualizing sense of self and have developed a pattern of experiencing life in a passive, submissive manner. They view themselves as helpless, hopeless victims of forces beyond their control.

"When I was growing up it was like I had no choice. I didn't know what to do and it seemed the only thing I could do was avoid people. It seemed like whatever I had to say didn't matter at all to anybody, especially my father."

They regard the world as hostile and uncaring, and interpret criticism as rejection, which adds to low self-esteem and poor self confidence.

"I realize now that I would react in a real bad way when anybody would make a comment to me that I thought was negative. But it seemed like I always heard things that were negative and so I guess that's what I really thought of myself."

Guilt

Most offenders feel guilty about their acts of sexual abuse, but don't know how to stop. Often they will attempt to hide behind the excuse of intoxication (see **Abuse of Alcohol and/or Drugs** on page 55), or use other rationalizations to justify their behavior.

"I remember that I touched my daughter probably about 60 or 70 times and a lot of those times we had intercourse. I usually felt really guilty about this and didn't know how to deal with it.

One day when I was in my room my daughter came in and sat on the same side of the bed and she grabbed my penis. I didn't know what to think of this except the first thing I thought was that everything I did in the past to my daughter was justified because she wanted it. I'm in treatment now and I want you to know that my daughter only did what I taught her to do. I found out later that day that my daughter broke up with her boyfriend and was feeling really hurt and only wanted to be loved and accepted. As she started doing that more often I even felt guiltier and I thought I had to start paying her, so I did. Usually after every time we had sex I would give her 20, 30 or 50 bucks. Later on I almost started to believe I was just buying a service."

Denial, or minimizing the impact of his abuse upon the victim is another technique the offender uses to deal with his guilt feelings.

"I thought to myself that if she never told me to stop or didn't fight back physically she must like it and want it. I remember saying to her once that she should turn me in to the police because I have this problem and I cannot stop."

In this case, the offender is able to justify his actions by placing the responsibility for them on the victim. This child was too young and too frightened to say anything about what was occurring. The offender was able to interpret her frightened silence as acceptance and even enjoyment of his abuse.

Isolation and Alienation from Others

Most offenders are lonely people; they experience an intense feeling of isolation and alienation from others, not only in their families, but with their peers as well. Their history of superficial interpersonal relationships makes it very difficult for them to establish and maintain meaningful relationships as adults.

"When I got married I didn't end the relationship by kicking my wife out like I did the other people. But I didn't provide her with any support or caring at all. I felt resentful towards her. It seemed the more she wanted to get close to me the more I wanted to push her away."

Often the offender will "play games" with his spouse in order to minimize the intimate contact with her, and rationalize the abuse of his child. Consider this example:

"I realized my wife wanted sex with me last night so I purposely went to bed late. When I got to bed she was already asleep, and when I began touching her, she asked me why I hadn't come to bed earlier and that right now she was too tired. I got up out of bed and left the room in a state of anger. I know that when I do that my wife is usually too frightened to come out, and most often just goes back to sleep. When she did that, I would then go down stairs and make some noise in the kitchen for her to think that I was down there watching TV or something. After about ten minutes or so I would go into my daughter's bedroom and start touching her. When I was touching her I was saying over and over in my mind, if my wife knew what I was doing she would never have rejected me and would have given me the sex that I wanted."

Low Awareness of Feelings

Most incest offenders are unable to differentiate what they think from what they feel. This has probably developed as a reaction to feeling judged, criticized and rejected when they disclosed self-related personal issues as a child. As a result, their ability to experience feelings of any kind is impaired.

"When I was really young I wanted to talk about how I felt when things would go wrong. But it seemed like nobody wanted to listen. I can remember a couple of times talking to my mom about how I felt about how dad treated her, but she shut that off real quick. It seemed like I learnt whenever I talked about feelings I had to be quiet because nobody wanted to listen. As I got older it seemed like I never wanted to talk about feelings any more because whenever I did it hurt so bad that I didn't know how to deal with that either because there was nobody I could go to to talk about what I felt. Until recently, I didn't realize that I had feelings, especially through my adult life. I'm thirty-five years old now, so I guess from the age of about twelve years 'til thirty-five years old I didn't feel anything. I'm learning now that I tend to talk more about what I think and what other people do than about anything that I ever feel. I'm beginning to see that this is a problem. I think that it's part of the problem why I started touching my daughter and my son sexually, that I couldn't feel the pain that they felt because I would block out feeling anything."

Many offenders, as children, went to extreme lengths to distance themselves from painful emotions they experienced. In order to suppress emotional pain, they often created anger.

"... and whenever I thought of it, I began to cry and break down. I was so afraid of doing this, that my only defence against it was to create anger. So what I would do was start hitting myself until it hurt and then I became so frustrated that the pain turned into anger. Once angry I was able to distance myself from the pain that I was experiencing."

Offenders may carry over this type of behavior into adulthood, creating anger to blot out pain.

Sexual Preoccupation

Many incest offenders are preoccupied with sex.

"It seems like I couldn't get sex out of my mind. Whenever a woman would walk by I would always look at her and imagine

what she would look like naked. It seemed at work all we ever did was joke around about sex. Over the last few years I can't remember a time or day going by without me ever thinking of that."

The Role of Fantasy

Fantasy plays an important role in the incest offender's ability to rationalize his abuse and continue with it. Many offenders fantasize about having a certain type of adult sexual relationship with the child. In the example below, the offender works hard to maintain a fantasy that his daughter is not really his daughter.

"Often I would just think of her as my wife even though, down deep, I realized that she was my daughter. I would pretend that she wasn't related to me and that she was either like a girlfriend or my wife. It really became hard to deal with at special occasions like my birthday or Christmas when she gave me a card and a gift and signed the card, 'Love your daughter, Angela'. I often would not read the card, which became pretty annoying to them; but, I don't think they ever caught on that if I read the card I would have to start looking at my daughter more as my daughter."

The offender also uses fantasy to convince himself that the victim approves of the abuse he is committing as in the two following cases:

"I guess I fantasized a bit about my daughter as well, because I use to pretend that she wanted what I was doing and that because she didn't tell, it meant that she liked it. I realize now that this is not true, but that is the rationale that I used in order to convince myself that it was okay."

"One time my daughter came out of the bedroom and she was wearing a real nice dress. She looked so grown up. I remember saying to myself that if she came over to me when I called her then she wanted me to touch her again. Touch her sexually, I mean. Well I called her over and she came to me so easily and I didn't even have to make her. She sat right on my knee. I also remember thinking that she knew that I was getting an erection and that she must of felt it. I am sure she must of. Anyway, I use to think about that situation lots of times. Over and over again I would play it back in my head. I use to do that kind of thing often. I lived in a real fantasy land."

Poor Sleeping Habits

Often the offender has poor sleeping habits which may result from an inability to distance himself from his problems. If he abuses his child during the evening, while bathing her or putting her to bed, for example, he may feel guilty and be unable to sleep for this reason.

"When I was a kid I used to sleep an awful lot to try and get away from my problems. When I was older I felt like I couldn't sleep at all. It seemed like whenever I would go to bed I would just be tossing and turning thinking about what was going wrong at home, what was going wrong at work and I just couldn't sleep. As a result I would go to work and I would be really tired in the morning but I would always give everything I had at work because there was no way I could lose my job. When I look back at it now, usually at nighttime it was the time when I sexually assaulted my daughter. I think that kept me awake quite a bit because before I touched her at night I would always think about how I was going to do it, and after I touched her I always thought about why I did it. Either way it seems like I never slept very good."

Inappropriate Relationship to the Victim

The offender frequently displays an inappropriate relationship to the child victim in one of several different ways. Often he displays favoritism towards the victim bestowing special gifts, priviledges or attention on her. This type of behavior arouses jealousy and resentment towards the victim from her mother and siblings. He may even deliberately promote hostility between his victim and her sibling(s) as is revealed in the following letter from an offender to his daughter whom he did not sexually assault.

Dear Caroline,

I know that you have wondered for a long time now why I touched your sister sexually and I never touched you. Well I'm beginning to understand the reason for this. Because your sister seemed very easy to touch in the sense that I thought she would never tell anybody. I realize that she was pretty much afraid of me and wasn't too able to talk to anybody about it.

You were kind of different, you seemed to always say what was on your mind. I was afraid that if I ever touched you, you would probably tell your mom about it or go and tell somebody else. I felt really scared about that and so I stayed away from you. You seemed to be a lot like I was, and I don't mean that in a bad way. You also had a pretty bad temper and you seemed to blurt things out without really thinking. I was afraid that if I touched you you might blurt out the fact that I was touching you to somebody and there was no way that I could have that. I realized that you and I probably wouldn't get very close together and I didn't want you to develop any real good relationship with your sister so I got angry at you and took out all my anger and frustration on you. I didn't take it out on your sister because I was afraid that if I treated her badly, by that I mean getting angry at her, that she would tell somebody what I was doing. So I treated her really nice and gave her things and money and stuff, in hopes that she wouldn't tell.

I realize that if I treated you badly that you would probably take out your frustration and anger on your sister and it looks like you did. I'm really sorry for all of that and I hope through this process that we can all understand it.
With my love,
Dad

In such an environment created by the offender, the child victim soon learns that she receives benefits from her involvement. It should be noted that this behavior and understanding is *learned* as a result of coercion by the offender.

In many cases the offender uses his relationship with the child victim as a substitute for peer relationships. For example, an incest offender will often discuss with his child, problems that he is experiencing with his spouse. He does this in the hope of receiving sympathy from the child which he then manipulates into a sense of obligation for the child to satisfy him sexually.

"I realize that my daughter was very protective of me and usually took my side when she saw her mom and I fighting. Quite often I would go to her and cry and she would hold me and I usually felt comforted. When she was holding me and trying to comfort me I most often turned that situation into something sexual. I realize that she felt obligated to follow through and that she was scared of hurting my feelings if she denied me."

The offender will often become very possessive of the child victim and want to completely monopolize her time. He may even experience jealousy at the child's attempts to have normal social relationships with her own peers. As a result, he may try to forbid these outside contacts and thereby inhibit the victim's ability to develop healthy, positive social skills.

"It wasn't only that I wanted to keep the secret; it was also that I felt really jealous when my daughter would spend time with anybody other than me. I thought at that time I did the only thing I could do and that was to stop it."

Frequently, the relationship goes beyond that of the child being a peer-substitute for the offender; when role-reversal takes place, she becomes a mother-substitute for him as in the example below:

"It seemed like my daughter meant a lot of different things to me. She had a lot of the qualities in her that I wanted and most of those qualities my wife didn't have. When I look back now, my daughter had more qualities like my mother than like my wife. But it seemed like I could relate to my daughter more than I could my wife. I would usually become really frustrated with my relationship with Candice (his wife) but my relationship with my daughter seemed to be smooth and at least in the beginning didn't seem to be wrong."

Rigid Moralistic Parenting Style

The offender often claims to have high moral values and to be a Christian living by the word of God. He will use the Bible as a weapon against his wife and children in order to dominate them, carrying over the relationships between husband and wife, and father and children, that he experienced as a child.

"When I first got married and started having children I swore I'd stay away from the Bible and all that religion. But when I started losing control of the family and my wife started taking over, we turned more to the Bible and religion and it seemed like the more we did, the more I got back my sense of power. I made my children obey it just like I was made to obey it when I was a kid, because it was the only thing they seemed to listen to. I realize now that I abused that and took something that was meant for good and only created evil."

Along with his image of himself as "head of the house", the offender often believes that he has "entitlement" to his wife and child victim; he refers to them and treats them like possessions. He tends to call the child victim by pet names rather than by her birth name; his wife he often refers to as "the wife" because this form of reference is impersonal and creates a sense of possession.

"Because my daughter was my daughter I thought that I owned her, I thought that I could get her to do anything I wanted and she should do it without question. Likewise, my wife, I thought because she got married to me, I became the boss and

that she was mine for me to do with as I saw fit."

Abusive Attitude Towards Power and Control

Most incest offenders have a very unhealthy attitude towards power and control. They can sometimes accept not having control in a structured environment like their work place, but home life presents a different problem.

"Work was pretty easy 'cause I was with the guys and you knew who the boss was. That's the guy getting paid for telling you what to do. It was easier to follow what was going on there than to do it at home. At work I wasn't always in a position of being the boss, but when I was it felt really good. Because I wasn't the boss most often at home, I had this need to be able to control people or to tell them what to do. So I started taking control of my family and ordering them around like I would be at work."

At home, the offenders often try to establish and maintain power and control over their families by intimidating them. Through verbally aggressive behavior, or even physical assault, they create a false powerful front with which they threaten family members.

"I had this need to feel like I was in control and the almighty powerful one in the family. Actually my wife was the dominant one, except when I got really mad. I hated being so angry all the time, but it was the only way in my mind that I could control her or take a stand. All I really wanted from them was to be accepted and not to be judged. I guess they didn't understand that. I know I surely didn't understand that. Maybe that's why we ended up in this mess."

Because the offender needs to view himself as a ruler or leader, he feels very threatened and becomes aggressive, sometimes to the point of violence when his pseudo-leadership is challenged. He will attempt to re-establish his control over his family through the use of fear tactics.

"I didn't know how to talk problems out and I didn't know how to express myself, especially I didn't know how to talk about feelings. The only thing I really knew what to do was to create a fear in my family. Whenever I felt like my position in the family was threatened or was going to be lost, I'd create this fear in them in order to be seen as the guy in control again."

Frequently the offender uses fear as his means of keeping secret the abuse he is committing.

"I was really afraid that somebody would find out about what was going on. The only way I could be assured that nobody would know was to stop my wife and children from ever going outside of the house. At one point I even thought that what I would do was pull my kids from school and get a tutor or something for them to learn at home so that they wouldn't be around their friends. I never did go that far but I created such a fear in my kids that there was no way they would ever bring kids home. I knew that as long as I had that fear in them, that the secret would be kept."

Abuse of Alcohol and/or Drugs

Frequently, individuals who commit incest or child sexual assault also have problems with alcohol and/or drug abuse. As we have seen from their psychological characteristics described above, offenders have low self-esteem, feel isolated and alienated from others, and feel powerless to control their lives. Because of this combination of feelings, they often tend to run away from problems rather than face them. The abuse of intoxicants provides another way of doing this.

Offenders also often use drugs or alcohol before, during or after committing sexual abuse. If they use drugs before the assault, they place the responsibility for their actions on the drug. They will make statements such as: "I would never have touched my child if I hadn't been drinking (or been stoned)." or "I can't remember what I did to you because I was drunk (or stoned)." It should be noted that the drug or alcohol is not responsible for the sexual abuse. The offender often consumes these substances with the full intent of sexually assaulting a child, only needing justification and the lowering of inhibitions. When offenders use drugs/alcohol after the assault, it is often an attempt to relieve the guilt they feel for what they have done.

Unrealistic Expectations of Self and Others

Most incest offenders set standards for themselves that are unrealistic and unattainable. When they fail to achieve these standards, their negative self image and sense of personal failure are reinforced. They may also fear success.

"I don't know whether or not I was more afraid of failing or if I was afraid of succeeding at something. I realize when I look back that I set real high expectations for myself that I never was able to meet. My dad always used to say to me, 'go for it all and if you don't make it you know that you're a failure' so I would always set standards for myself that were real high. I'd go for it and I would always fail.

In the same way that offenders are unrealistic in their
expectations of themselves, they often impose unrealistically high
standards on the members of their families as well.

Hostility or Aloofness Towards Family of Origin

Because of the unhappy relationship the offender has had with
his own family of origin, he is usually quite reluctant to spend any
time with them. His attitude may range from aloofness to his
parents and siblings, to outright hostility. Feeling isolated from
his own family, he may try to impose similar isolation onto his
wife, forbidding her to maintain the contact she wishes with her
parents and siblings.

Types of Sexually Abusive Behavior

Individual offenders may engage in any, or all, or any combination of the following types of abuse.

Incidental Fondling

Often as the first form of sexual contact, the offender fondles the victim through incidental forms of contact. For example, he may use play wrestling with his child as a cover for brushing against or fondling his child's breasts or vaginal area, or if it's a male, his penis.

"Quite often I would wrestle around with my kids, usually giving an impression to my wife that we were having fun. I would use this way of touching them. It was easy to make it look like I accidentally fondled her breast when in fact I did it purposely. Likewise I would grab her on the leg and my hand would accidentally on purpose slip up and touch her vagina. It seemed sometimes that that's all I needed to do but I can't understand why one time that's all I'd need and other times I'd need to have sex."

Extensive Fondling

Many offenders become involved in their children's hygiene and willingly accept the responsibility of putting their children to bed at night. Bathing their children gives offenders the opportunity to do vaginal, breast, anal and penal inspections and fondling. Similarily, tucking their children into bed provides additional opportunities to fondle them without raising suspicion.

"My wife was always hounding me to take more interest in the kids. It wasn't her fault that I sexually assaulted the kids but because she kept hounding me to be more involved with them, talk to them and to read them stories, I decided to use that way to sexually assault my kids. What I would do was put them to bed at night and that was usually a time when my wife would leave us alone and I would touch my kids sexually."

Voyeurism

In order to continue the fantasy most offenders hold in respect to touching their children sexually, many try to watch their children when they are naked or in the process of dressing.

Viewing their children this way provides a fantasy for them which reinforces the sexual acts and helps rationalize the abuse. Some offenders go as far as drilling holes in the floor, or devising other methods to view their children's nudity.

"My daughter's bedroom was right below the front room area. Actually it was right below my chair where I used to sit in the front room. One time when the kids and my wife were gone I drilled a hole underneath the carpet from the front room down to her bedroom. It was right in an area where I could see her when she was changing. What I would do was watch her while she changed clothes and I would usually do this at times when my wife was out bowling or playing bingo or something. I can remember it got to the point where I would encourage my wife to go out and do more things. She thought I was being real nice when really what I wanted was to be able to watch my daughter."

Use of Pornography

Some offenders use pornography or sexually related literature to coerce the child. For example, the offender may show the child pictures from magazines that display naked women or men posing or engaging in sexual acts. Generally, the child's response is one of discomfort but usually they are unsure as to how to react. The offender is able to interpret this as the child accepting his behavior.

"I used to buy a lot of pornographic magazines, you know the kind that show women and men doing all sorts of sexual things to each other. I'd leave these things lying around the house and sometimes I would actually sit down with my daughter and at times her friends too, and show them the pictures. I really wanted to find out what they would do and how they would react to seeing those pictures. That's why I showed it to them. Some of the kids would act like it was really dirty and terrible, I knew that those kids weren't the ones for me to touch. The other ones that acted kind of giggly and funny and made jokes about it, I realized that they probably wouldn't tell anybody if I touched them."

"Cruising"

Some incest offenders will "cruise" the streets in their cars or have their children bring home their peers in order to gain access to them. Often these offenders have difficulty accounting for their time or explaining their whereabouts.

"I used to tell my wife that I got off at work at 5:00, I really got

off work at 3:30. What I would do usually after work was drive around the school yards and recreation centers and places like that to take a look at the kids who were there. I never really wanted to touch them sexually but I really looked at the differences between how they were built. The only person I ever did touch sexually in an abusive way, I mean, is my daughter. It would bother me when my wife would ask me what I did with my free time. I thought that maybe she knew that I was driving around the school yards and playgrounds and I never touched anybody. I thought she was trying to accuse me of touching people, when in fact I didn't do it."

Disguising Abuse as "Sex Education"

Often the offender will view himself as the sex educator of the family. He may use the guise of sex education as an excuse to engage in sexual acts with them.

"At one time I sat down with my daughter and son and told them that it was time they started learning about the facts of life. They seemed to be interested in learning it and I used their body parts and my body parts to point out the differences. At one time I got my daughter to masturbate me to show her the difference between a penis with an erection and one without it. My daughter giggled and laughed when she did this and well, from there things just continued."

Exhibitionism

Incest offenders are often exhibitionists who tend to flaunt their bodies with the desire of arousing the child or others.

"I got my child to model her bathing suit for me. I gave her lots of praise and compliments, which I knew she liked. After she showed me what she looked like in her bathing suit I went and put mine on. Before I put mine on though, I masturbated to the point of getting an erection. The bathing suit that I had was a bikini bathing suit, and when I wore it, it was obvious that I had an erection. I did this purposefully with the hope that my daughter would look at the erection and become aroused."

Offenders may also expose themselves to their children by leaving their bedroom door or bathroom door open when changing or at other times when their children are likely to see them unclothed.

Intercourse

Many offenders engage in intercourse, vaginal, anal, or both, with their victims. Anal intercourse is a common form of abuse for males; girls are subject to both anal and vaginal intercourse.

The offender may have a premeditated preference in respect to types of sexual abuse as in the following case:

"The sexual abuse of my daughter really consisted of fondling her breasts and her vagina. It was my son who I had anal intercourse with."

In some cases, the offender engages in anal intercourse with a girl victim in order to eliminate the possibility of making her pregnant.

"I was really afraid that I would get my daughter pregnant if we had intercourse in the normal way, and she was really scared that she would get pregnant too. So, to eliminate any chance of this, I had anal intercourse with her because that way she couldn't get pregnant."

Oral Sex

Some offenders perform oral sex on the child victim and/or demand that the victim perform oral sex on the offender. The offender may feel an even greater sense of power and domination through coercing oral sex, than from other forms of sexual activity, as in this case.

"... The only thing that I can say is the power I felt is why I did it. When I made my daughter kneel down in front of me to commit oral sex, it was like a rush of power went through me. It was like I controlled someone and they had to do as I said. No-one else ever did as I would say so usually I never felt like that. But during those times I felt powerful and in control...."

Chapter 5
Characteristics of a
Non-offending Parent

Introduction

The non-offending parent (mother, unless otherwise indicated) like her abusing spouse, generally comes from an unhappy past riddled with abuse, failure experiences, ridicule and condemnation. Frequently, she herself is a victim of past sexual abuse and carries within her all the trauma that that implies.

Many non-offending spouses enter marriage hoping that their spouse will provide them with the nurturance and security that was lacking in their family of origin.

Yet, without realizing it, they often seek a partner who has some of the same characteristics and qualities as their non-nurturing and absent parents or caretakers.

Like her husband, the mother in the incestuous family tends to lack any sense of comfort, security, direction and happiness in life, and is often tormented by unresolved issues from her past.

"Now that I've had an opportunity to look at my own life and the relationship of my husband and children, I've come to realize a number of things. The way that I acted throughout my marriage was very self-centered and it seems like I did most of the things that I accused my husband of doing.

When I look back at my mom and her mom, I have had a chance to do that, they really weren't any different than I was. It seems like my grandmother taught my mother to be the type of woman she is and in turn my mom taught me. It's like we are puppets allowing other people to pull the strings that control us.

When I first learnt about this I was really angry because the first thing that I lost was my ability to blame other people for doing that to me. As it turns out I allowed them to do it. Initially that was more painful to admit than it is now. I see it now that as a child I didn't have much of a choice but when I started growing up and became an adult, I'm sure now that I chose the path that I ended up on."

Psychological Characteristics

Low Self-Esteem

In terms of her low self-esteem and negative self image, the non-offending parent is very similar to her abusive husband and abused daughter. She usually has not learned to deal with problems effectively, or express her feelings in a healthy and responsible manner. She is often insecure, has difficulty making decisions, and has learned to react to life in an unassertive manner, accepting whatever is "dished out" to her. Within the incestuous family she plays a passive, subordinate role, and feels incapable of making changes within her own life.

"I realize that my husband saved me from a lousy marriage and relationship before and I felt obligated to do what it was he wanted me to do. It seemed like every time I wanted to voice my own opinion, he would shoot that down quicker than anything. After a while I just thought that my opinion and actually me, myself was just useless."

The childhood and adolescence of the non-offending parent are generally characterized by experiences that have reinforced a negative self image.

"For most of my life I have felt pretty much as a nothing. It seems like my dad and especially my mom didn't do anything about trying to change that for me. The boyfriends that I've had for some reason had been able to see that in me, because for a while things would go along fine but after that they treated me like I was a piece of nothing. In my latter teenage years after people had been taking advantage of me for a long time, I started not to care too much about myself. In fact I cared so little that I started doing things to other people before they had a chance to do them to me. What I mean by this is sometimes I would dump them or treat them like nothing before they had a chance to treat me like that."

In order to protect herself from additional rejection and pain, this person adapted by deliberately destroying relationships.

As a result of her low self-confidence and impaired emotional and psychological growth, the mother in the incestuous family experiences overwhelming fears of becoming a single parent. In her desperation to preserve the security she experiences from her role in the home, even if she feels abused there, she often denies the many problems within her family.

"When I was a little girl I used to see the problems that my mom had, going from relationship to relationship. It seemed like she was always getting deeper and deeper into trouble. One time I asked her why she doesn't stay with one person and she said that when I get older I would understand. As I started getting older I realized that I too was going from relationship to relationship. However each relationship, even though it seemed like a lifetime, really only lasted a few months or a couple of years at the most. In the last relationship, the one with Ken, I began to develop an intense fear that I might become a single parent. We have four children, all of which are under the age of nine. I just couldn't handle looking after them all by myself. Ken isn't around an awful lot but that doesn't seem to matter when it comes to being alone completely. I guess I'm one of those women who would rather do whatever she is told, whenever she is told, however she is told, instead of being by herself."

Guilt

Most mothers of victims lack the strength, understanding and resourcefulness to respond effectively to the dysfunction in their incestuous families. Their fears of separation, change, and revenge from the offender, interfere with and overpower their ability to take affirmative measures to end the abuse.

Such a mother may have ignored her child's cries for help even to the point of not reacting appropriately to an actual disclosure of abuse. Instead, she may have tried to escape from family pressures and responsibilities in order to minimize the risk to herself. As a result, the mother of the incest victim frequently feels guilty about having "failed to protect her child."

Isolation and Alienation from Others

The non-offending parent shares with her abusive husband and victimized daughter, an extreme sense of loneliness and isolation. She is very likely hostile towards her own family of origin in which she was probably sexually abused. She often feels particularly resentful of her mother, with whom she has experienced role reversal as a child and been forced to accept responsibilities well beyond her years.

"I remember she (mother) seemed to never let me live as a child. Whenever I would play with toys she would take them away from me and tell me to 'grow up.' I was washing dishes, cleaning the house, looking after laundry and making my father's lunches on a daily basis before I was eight years old. It seemed I felt an obligation to have to do these things and the more I did it the more

it seemed my dad became dependent on it. It seemed a natural progression that my father and I would then become involved sexually. As that seemed to me, back then, the only need of his I wasn't meeting."

The mother is also isolated within her present family. She feels jealous, distrusting and hostile towards her daughter and is threatened by the incestuous relationship between her daughter and husband. Because of these feelings she is very critical of her daughter in a way which further isolates the two of them from each other.

"I thought she was out to get me. I literally thought that my daughter was trying to make me jealous and take my husband away from me. I was astounded at the things that she would do and felt I had no other choice but to get back at her."

In addition to her alienation from her family of origin and her present family, the mother in the incestuous family often has few supportive peer relationships. Frequently, she has been coerced by the offender to minimize her social contacts outside the family, and she feels trapped in a life of imprisonment.

"It seemed like I couldn't go anywhere. Whenever I would want to do anything, like get a job or do some volunteer work, my husband would always be so threatened and he would get angry and frustrated. At times I had to just walk away from developing a new relationship with somebody because I knew it would always end. I realize now that I could have stood up for myself and done something about it, but back then I just felt like my husband controlled me."

Problems of Sexual Identity

The non-offending parent frequently has problems with her own sexual identity. This often stems, at least in part, from her own past history of abuse.

"For most of my life the people who touched me also sexually were women. When I was really young, about how old my daughter is now, (16 years) I remember liking this one girl and we began seeing each other. Before we knew it we were both involved with each other in a sexual way. I began to think that if a female touched me sexually it must mean that I am gay. So I tried for the longest time to force myself to like women sexually."

In some cases, the mother may be from a background that was

not only sexually abusive, but one in which she has learned almost nothing at all about the nature of sexuality.

"It seems like I'm trying to address most things that happened in my life. One area, though, still really bothers me. That's the fact that neither my mom nor older sister sat down with me and really talked to me about sex. Believe it or not I got pregnant when I was 16 years old and I didn't know how I got pregnant. My father was the one who got me pregnant. He told my mom that it was something that my boyfriend did to me to get me pregnant. Everybody assumed that I knew what my boyfriend should have done to me that got me pregnant, but I didn't. They went and took me to a doctor who gave me an abortion and the only thing that I said to him was that my boyfriend got me pregnant. After the abortion I thought I would stay right away from boys for fear that I would get pregnant again. But I didn't know what I was running away from because I would even avoid walking in a different direction down a street for fear I might get pregnant passing one of them. I know this probably sounds really crazy, but if you think it sounds crazy to you, you should see what it sounds like to me.

To top it off, when I was 20 years old, I moved away from home, I met a man who was about 50 years old and we started to really like each other. As a result of that relationship I got pregnant again and again at the very beginning I didn't know how I got pregnant. It wasn't until I attended counselling for the past sexual abuse that somebody told me how I got pregnant."

The mother in the incestuous family may believe (as a result of accusations from her husband) that she is frigid, and that this is the cause of her husband's abuse of her daughter. (See **Rationalization** on page 70.)

"I knew all along that my husband wanted sex from me, but it seemed that it was the only thing I had left that I could control. When he would touch me I would feel cold and clammy and I wouldn't be able to respond to him in a manner in which he wanted or actually, for that matter, in a way that I wanted to as well. I began to think that I wasn't able to be sexually aroused any more and used to view myself as being frigid. Actually my husband would accuse me quite often of being frigid and would often threaten that he would look for another woman if I wasn't able to give him what he wanted and as he said, what a man deserved."

Physical Ailments

Often, the non-offending parent suffers from physical ailments, usually created by an inability to deal with emotional issues. The ill health frequently places her in hospital or out of the family home for extended periods of time, giving the offender increased access to the child. If the mother is aware of this, she may deal with this knowledge in an unhealthy manner which results in additional physical illness, again removing her from the home.

"I couldn't handle the thought of what was occurring between my husband and daughter. It seemed that every time I thought about it I would get sick. I didn't realize back then that there may have been a connection between me getting sick and what I was dealing with emotionally. In looking back I would have to say that the first thing I thought of when I was under stress was the fact that I was going to get sick. Sure enough I got sick."

Blaming

The non-offending spouse often avoids responsibility for her own actions by blaming others, particularly her husband.

"My last relationship before I got married to this guy was really physically abusive. In one group that I was attending, I was taught that everything my first husband did to me was his fault and actually the responsibility for the marriage breakdown was his fault. When I got married to Brian, that's the guy I'm married to now, I brought along the attitude that whatever would go wrong in this marriage would be Brian's fault. I'm finding it hard to break that attitude, the blaming one. That is because I've lived such a long time blaming everybody else for the things that I've done."

Prior to the disclosure of the abuse, the mother may also blame herself for problems in the family. Once the abuse is disclosed, however, she may try to escape any responsibility by placing all the blame on her husband.

"Before my daughter disclosed the sexual abuse it seemed like I was responsible for everything that went wrong in my family, but after she told the police what my husband was doing, all the

focus for the destruction of our family seemed to be placed on him. I viewed that back then as an opportunity to alleviate some of the guilt and frustration that I had about being a slave in the family. I found it really difficult to focus on any of the problems that I had because everybody was talking to me about how bad my husband was. I started running him down and actually even created him to be more of a monster than he actually was. I saw this as an opportunity to rid myself of any of the blame and responsibility for what happened. When I thought about what my husband did to my daughter I felt so guilty like I had done something wrong. When everybody was blaming him it was really easy to accept that he was responsible because if he wasn't responsible then maybe I was."

Reaction to the Abuse

Often the non-offending parent realizes that there is something unhealthy about the relationships in the family, but refuses to look deeper for fear of what she might find. (See **Defence Mechanisms**, on the next page.) She wishes to avoid the responsibility of having to react if she finds anything severely unhealthy or dysfunctional.

Sometimes it is impossible for the mother to pretend that she does not know what is going on because the child has told her explicitly that sexual abuse is occurring. Upon hearing this, the mother reacts in one of many different ways. In some cases, she will respond in a healthy and supportive manner, accepting the child's disclosure and taking control of the situation to stop the abuse from continuing.

Some may try to stop the abuse by confronting the offender in the hope that he will admit and stop the abusive behavior. Or, they may try to protect the child by preventing her from being alone with the offender.

Others may accept the child's disclosure, but after considering the family situation and the risk of responding, ignore the allegations and act as if nothing had occurred.

Still others may disbelieve the child and react with hostility and anger, warning the child never to discuss the matter again.

In some cases, the mother knows what is going on but because of her own sense of anger, betrayal and helplessness, she responds to it in a very unhealthy, dysfunctional manner.

"I became so outraged at the thought that my husband and my child were having an affair. It was like I was living with another woman in the family and I felt this strong urge to get back at her for what she was stealing from me. I remember once when I was going out of the home for the evening, I think it was to a bingo game, that I thought to myself, that my husband and daughter

---

are probably going to have an affair. So I went to my husband and said to him, that if you think that I'm going to have sex with you tonight you better think again, so you may as well look elsewhere. As I walked out of the room I turned towards my daughter, who was sitting on the couch near my husband, and I said to her,'I hope you enjoy what you get from him because I surely don't.'"

It is clear that the mother in this case knows that incest is occurring between her husband and daughter, but her inappropriate response to it actually encourages the abuse to continue.

Defence Mechanisms

In order to function within an incestuous family, the non-offending spouse develops a strong set of defence mechansims. As you read through these, you will probably see many similarities between her methods of coping and those of the victim and incest offender.

Denial

Denial is a simple refusal to accept the reality of actual events. For example, the mother may make statements like "I'm sure that didn't really occur," or "I am not an alcoholic," or "I am sure he did not touch my child sexually."

"When I first heard from the police that my husband was being suspected of sexually assaulting my daughter I didn't know what to do. He seemed like such a good man and our marriage seemed so good. After I was finally able to accept that my husband did sexually assault my daughter I also was able to accept that our marriage was terrible and that my husband really was a very abusive man."

Minimizing

In a response that is closely related to denial, the mother will often minimize in her own mind, the degree of dysfunction and unhealthiness of the family, and the extent of her own abuse. She does this with statements like: "I was only assaulted once," or "He didn't hit me all that often," or "Well, he never had intercourse with her did he?"

Minimizing is an effective but unhealthy way for the non-offending parent to avoid responsibility for reacting or making changes to an abusive situation.

"I didn't think that Kim's uncle touching her twice would be any big deal for her. I was touched at least twice in a sexual way when I was a child and it didn't do anything to me."

Repression/Selective Memory

Often the non-offending parent has learned to repress or forget events that she has viewed as threatening or undesirable, and carries this behavior over into her adult life. She remembers only what she chooses because if she remembers all, she would experience pain, anxiety and frustration. She makes statements like: "I don't recall whether anybody did that to me," or "I'm not sure whether or not that happened; I can't remember." One of the things she has probably chosen to forget, is her own past history of abuse.

"Until the social worker came and talked to me about my daughter's sexual abuse I hadn't even remembered that I was sexually assaulted as a child. Now that we are going through treatment with my daughter, my own past issues tend to be coming up around every corner."

Even though her memory is selective, she still suffers from the events she is repressing. When her issues emerge, she has to deal not only with the issues themselves, but also with her past denial of them.

"All I can remember about my life before disclosure is that I had a very bad memory. It seemed like everything would cost so much if I was to remember it. So I simply chose at times not to. After a while I couldn't remember whether I chose to do that or whether or not I really didn't remember and it became so confusing to me. After my daughter disclosed the sexual abuse and we started getting treatment, the first thing I noticed was my memory starting to come back. At first it was really painful because I really wished I would have forgotton some of those things but after the pain was dealt with the risk of remembering was gone."

Withdrawal

Often, the non-offending parent copes through withdrawal. Sometimes this is done through physical withdrawal from the home, as in cases when she develops outside interests, or takes a job in order to escape the family environment.

"The more I became jealous of the relationship between my

daughter and her father the more outraged and desperate I became. It didn't seem like I could do anything about their relationship except get away from it. So I began to develop outside interests. When I first started doing that it really seemed to threaten Larry (her husband) because at times he used to say to me that he would beat me up or do something to me if I didn't stay at home. But I just had to get away and it was the only way I knew of to deal with the situation. I look at that now as running, but back then it seemed running was the only thing I was good at."

Unfortunately, this reaction usually creates additional anxiety and anger within her husband who views this as a loss of power and control over her. It also creates distance between the mother and daughter which then reduces the likelihood that the child will disclose the abuse.

In other instances of withdrawal, like the one described below, the non-offending parent may simply retreat into silence.

"It seemed like I didn't have many choices. It was either stay there and fight or pull out. I chose to pull out. Athough I never left the house physically, my mind and my emotions were gone."

The child may view either form of withdrawal, physical or emotional, as rejection, and as encouraging of the abusive behavior.

Rationalization

The non-offending spouse tends to rationalize her husband's behavior by making comments such as: "My husband touched my daughter because I didn't give him sex," or "I drove him to drinking," or "My child made me do that to her."

Here is a specific case of a mother rationalizing her husband's abuse of her daughter.

"After hearing that my daughter was touched sexually I felt so guilty. It must have been something I had done that made my husband want to touch my daughter. I didn't think the fact that we didn't have sex that often would make him do something like that."

In actual fact, the husband's abuse of their daughter has nothing to do with whether or not this woman had sex with him.

Fantasy

The non-offending parent often tries to live in a fantasy world in which she has much more control than she does in her real world. She makes comments like "If only I could...", or "If only he would..."

"It seemed like I was living in two different worlds, the world of my choice and the world with my husband and family. In the world of my choice I could do anything I wanted to, and be anything I wanted. People there treated me kind and helped me to understand. In the real world, things were opposite to my fantasies."

Procrastination

When the non-offending parent learns of the sexual abuse, possibly through her daughter telling her, she may procrastinate for long periods of time before doing anything about it. She may say "I'll talk to them tomorrow," or "I'll tell somebody about this sometime, I'm just not sure when."

"I really don't remember how many times my daughter told me about the sexual abuse. I do remember though that each time she told me I promised her I would do something about it. Each time I promised her she looked so much happier that I thought she would just forget. The way I dealt with this with my daughter was basically the way I dealt with everything in my life. I had this belief that if I could put it off until next year don't ever bother trying to do it today."

Resistance

Often the mother wishes to maintain distance between herself and the victim. Through the use of anger, denial or aggression, she blocks the victim's approach and creates situations where her daughter is unable to disclose the sexual abuse to her.

"At times I knew my daughter was going to talk to me about something. I didn't really know that it was about sexual abuse but I knew that it was about something that was bothering her. I had so many problems of my own that I seemed to create an image for my daughter, especially my daughter, that said to her I don't want to listen. I guess that's what hurts so much now. I really did want to listen, but I know the image I created was, 'I don't want to hear what you have to say.'"

Reaction Formation

The non-offending spouse often fakes her feelings in order to project to others an image of what she would like her family to be. To outside people she may appear calm, collected and in control.

Inside, however, she may feel extremely confused and insecure, and be seething with rage.

"To everybody else it really seemed like I was a calm, cool person who could deal with most everybody's problems. I guess they thought that because I would always go to people and help them and I was a pretty good listener. However, inside I had so much rage and anger and thought many times to end it all."

Anger

Despite the non-offending parent's often passive behavior, her anger sometimes erupts to the surface, or is consciously used to influence the behavior of members of her family.

"One of the biggest complaints I had about my husband is that he had such an angry violent temper. When I look back on my own life it seemed like I played the same game I accused him of. I would either let him walk all over me or I would blow my top. When I let him walk all over me it seems he would always walk over me and be angry. However, when I blew my top he always became really passive and let me walk over him. Sooner or later it became such a vicious circle I just hoped some time it would end."

Like the victim and the incest offender, the non-offending parent also uses anger in order to repress or deny painful emotions.

"Whenever the reality of what was happening to my daughter came true for me, I felt very upset, hurt and didn't know how to deal with it. I soon learnt that if I became angry at my daughter the painful feelings went away and I no longer had to address them."

Chapter 6

Characteristics of the Sibling(s)
of an Incest Victim

Introduction

Often the siblings of victims of incest or child sexual abuse are overlooked and forgotten during the investigation of the incestuous family. Investigators may believe that because the siblings were not sexually victimized, that they have not been traumatized.

This belief is mistaken; siblings share many of the same problems and symptoms as those of the victim, offender and non-offending spouse. They play an important part in the dynamics and structure of the incestuous family.

"When my sister finally told about what was going on it seemed like nobody cared about me any more. That doesn't mean that they cared a lot about me before, because I don't think they did. But they didn't even ask me what was going on or how I felt about what was happening. I had been sexually assaulted by a couple of people also and I was waiting to see how they handled my sister's situation before I would tell them. When my sister first told someone I thought for sure somebody would come and ask me if somebody touched me. But nobody did. I don't know, maybe they don't think boys could be touched sexually and feel hurt about it. But even though I was touched sexually I think that I need just as much help as everybody else does, even if I wasn't touched. My dad, my mom, treated me just as badly as they treated everybody else. Just because they didn't touch me sexually doesn't mean I wasn't touched by somebody else and even if I wasn't it doesn't mean I don't need help."

The siblings, like the victim, offender and non-offending parent need treatment in order to understand what has occurred in their families. They, too, are usually unable to differentiate between what they think and what they feel, and cannot make much sense of their experience.

Without the understanding that comes from intensive therapy, they tend to grow up seeking relationships which are typical of those in the unhealthy and dysfunctional families from which they have come. As a result, they may take out the frustrations caused by the unresolved problems they experienced in their families of origin, on the new families they create for themselves, thus perpetuating a pattern of unhealthy, dysfunctional family relationships.

Characteristics of Siblings

Low Self-Esteem

The siblings of victims of incest or child sexual abuse share the low self-esteem and negative self image that is typical of all the members of the incestuous family. They too have experienced the offender's abusive attitudes towards power and control, sometimes to an even greater extent than the victim or mother.

"I was so jealous and resentful of the fact that my sister was getting all the attention that I just had to find ways to get back at her. I knew something wasn't right between her and my dad, but most of the times it just seemed like I didn't care. I really resented the fact that they spent so much time together and my dad barely looked at me except to yell at me. It seemed like I couldn't do anything right when I was around my dad 'cause he would always criticize me and make me feel like I was useless. He seemed to treat my sister with favors and would always give her things, but me he never gave anything. I can never recall him saying that he loved me or compliment me if I did something right. Actually it seemed like I lived most of my life without a dad."

In other cases, the sibling does not feel singled out for bad treatment, but recognizes that the whole family is being abused by the offender.

"I was really surprised that my sister was being abused sexually by my father. He didn't seem to treat her any different than he did me or my other brother and sister. He treated us all like crap. He would yell at us and scream at us. When he was drunk he would even do more. When my sister first told somebody about the sexual abuse I became really jealous because she got all the attention. I kept saying to myself, 'Doesn't everybody know that I feel just as lousey as she does?' But it didn't seem like anybody cared."

Guilt

If siblings have been told by the incest victim that the sexual abuse is occurring, they may feel very guilty for not stopping it. They may experience these intense guilt feelings even when they are younger than the victim, and have no idea how to stop the abuse.

"My sister came to me and told me that my dad was touching her sexually. I couldn't believe it. I couldn't believe that my dad would do something like that. I told her that she was a liar and that if she says things like that any more I would tell on her. She never did come back to me and tell me any more, but as I found out later my dad did continue to sexually abuse her. I guess the worst thing that I have to deal with right now is the fact that I feel so guilty that I didn't stop it."

Isolation and Alienation from the Family

The siblings of incest victims often experience an even greater sense of isolation from the family than the victim herself. One reason for this is the sibling's perception of a "special relationship" between the victim and the offender. The sibling(s) may not be aware that sexual abuse is occurring, but the favoritism often expressed by the offender towards the victim makes the sibling(s) feel ostracised from the family, frustrated, angry, and resentful towards, and jealous of, the victim.

"It was like I didn't even belong to the family. I didn't realize at the beginning that my sister was being sexually abused by my dad, but I knew that something was different between the two of them than between my dad and I. Even though I know now, I didn't know at the time that my sister was trying to protect me from my dad. When I kept pushing her away and telling her that I didn't need her help she became really defensive. When she became that way I had to get back at her and the only way I knew how to do it was to get really angry and scream and yell at her."

Sometimes, even the knowledge that the victim is being sexually abused contributes to the anger, resentment and jealousy felt towards the victim by the sibling(s).

"When I first found out that my dad was touching my sister, I became really angry. At first I had this strong need to deny it because I thought that if I accepted it, then I really wondered why my dad wouldn't want to touch me. That may sound stupid but I was actually feeling a bit resentful and jealous. After I was able to get over those feelings, I just wanted to deny that my dad would do something like that and I began to protect him. I realize that in saying those things I was hurting my sister, but I was finally getting some attention and some recognition and I was afraid of letting go of it. The more I denied it the more attention I got. And I hadn't had attention in the family for a long, long time."

Often the siblings of incest victims, like the victims themselves and the non-offending parents, respond to the alienation and dysfunctional relationships in the family through many of the defense mechanisms described for the non-offending parent. Withdrawal is one of the most common means of escape. The sibling may try to lead a separate life away from the family by developing outside interests.

"I'm not really sure why but we would always argue and fight. Nobody really cared about how the other person felt and when everybody was really hurting that seemed to be when everybody hurt each other more. I didn't know how to deal with it so I just had to get away from the house and away from my family. My dad really got angry at that and actually so did my mom. Each time I kept on going away my sister kept saying to me the further I go the better it would be. I don't know what she meant by that but I think it had something to do with my dad."

If the offender, through intimidation, disallows the development of appropriate peer/social relationships, the siblings will often withdraw into themselves, through escape to their rooms or by other means.

The Sibling as Victim

The alienation that the children in the incestuous family feel towards one another makes it easy for the offender to abuse all of them without the children knowing that any of their siblings are being abused. The offender will tell one child that if she permits the abuse, he will not abuse any of her siblings. He may then do the same thing to all the children in his family.

"There were six of us living in the family, four girls and two boys. The craziest thing about the whole thing is that my dad was sexually assaulting all of us and nobody knew about it, not even the other kids. I found out later that he told the same thing to everybody. He told me that if I told my brothers or sisters about what was going on he was going to sexually assault them. After I talked to my brothers and sisters when Lynn finally went and told somebody about it, we found out he said the same thing to everybody."

Sometimes, the sibling is concealing sexual abuse that he or she has experienced outside the family. When this is the case, the sibling and victim may be able to share their experiences of abuse as a means of supporting each other.

"After I told my brother that my dad was sexually assaulting

me, he seemed to understand. I realize he couldn't do anything about it but when he told me that somebody had touched him sexually, I was really surprised. At first I didn't realize that boys were touched sexually, but after he told me how he felt, I could really relate. It seemed like we had something in common and even though it didn't make it any easier to deal with what my dad was doing to me, it did seem to help knowing that my brother understood."

Chapter 7
The Incestuous Family

After looking at the characteristics of the individuals who make up an incestuous or sexually abusive family, one can see how the pattern of incest (or alcoholism, or physical abuse) can develop; it grows out of the self concepts and emotional needs of the parents who created the family.

It is not purely a matter of chance that these adults, the incest offender and his non-offending spouse find each other when they choose a mate. They deliberately seek the kind of spouse who will meet their needs and confirm the images they hold of themselves. These needs and self images, however, are basically unhealthy; they are the product of the abusive backgrounds from which both parents have come. Both partners are seeking a sense of acceptance, love and caring. However, their experiences in their families of origin make it difficult for them to establish healthy adult relationships.

Thus, a man who has learned abusive power relationships in his family of origin, and who consequently needs to feel dominant and controlling, will seek a wife who will be passive and submissive. Similarly, a woman who has learned to passively submit to the abusive power and authority of her father, including in most cases, to sexual abuse from him, will unconsciously seek a husband who will dominate and control her.

And so these damaged adults get together in a dysfunctional relationship, which substantiates for both of them, the unhealthy attitudes and feelings they hold. Husband and wife become bound to each other by their insecurities and unhealthy dependencies; each fears separation from the other.

When children are born, the parents are unable to respond to them and nurture them in a way that promotes a sense of security and health and the development of close loving relationships. Instead, the children are shaped by the low self-esteem, negative self images and unhealthy power relationships of their parents.

The unwritten rules within the incestuous family tend to be very strict and rigidly enforced. Any disobedience to the rules is a threat to the family, and especially to the power and control of the offender and the secrecy he requires. Consequently, the members of the incestuous family tend to alienate themselves from the outside world, and create an heirarchy within their own family system.

For their own reasons, all the members of the incestuous family strive to keep secret the abuse that is going on within it. The victim, for example, may keep the secret because she fears destroying the family and is afraid of what others will think of her. The non-offending parent (mother) may fear disclosure because she feels insecure and unable to cope with the possibility of becoming a single parent. The siblings of the family may not disclose because they don't know how to handle the situation, or because they are afraid to become involved. And, of course, the offender does not disclose for fear of the consequences to himself, of doing so.

As a result of these fears, the whole family often becomes united in warding off any outside influences on the family, or official involvement with it.

Without intervention, however, the children in the incestuous family become locked into a pattern of low self-esteem, negative self image, and unhealthy attitudes towards power and control in adult relationships. Whether they are sexually victimized or not, they often become adults like their parents, shaped in a way which will tend to perpetuate the cycle of abuse.

Chapter 8
From Their Own Mouths:
Personal Testimony of Members of Incestuous Families

In order to understand the thoughts and feelings, the pain, trauma and devastation that occurs as the result of incest or child sexual abuse, it is necessary to hear it from the mouths of the people involved.

This section further elaborates on the words of a number of individuals whose lives have been affected by dysfunctional and incestuous relationships, through their letters to other members of their families.

This first example was written by a twelve year old boy to his father. Mike had been sexually assaulted over a period of two years by his father, mother, aunt and older sister.

Dear Daddy
Please don't be mad at me for saying these things to you. I hurt inside my heart for how you hurt me like you did. Why did you hurt me like that? Didn't you love me? I did nice things for you but then you made me do sex on you. I thought you liked me when you did that because you told me that that was the way, but that was wrong. I think that you lied to me. How come you lied to me? Someday I will see you again and I must know whether you will ever do that to me again because if you will dad I cannot see you again. I miss you daddy and I feel so sorry for saying these things to you, but you need to know how I feel inside.
Bye daddy,
Mike

Incest had been occurring in Mike's family for generations. However, it was not revealed until Mike was able to disclose the abuse to a counsellor at school. Mike's father, mother, aunt and older sister had told him that the reason they were touching him sexually was because they loved him, wanted to show their affection and caring for him, and also because no one provided for them the same feelings. Mike indicated that he felt sorry for them and only wanted to make them happy. After viewing a television program, Mike questioned whether or not those activities were right or wrong; consequently, he discussed the situation with his counsellor. It was later discovered that Mike's mother, aunt and sister had been involved sexually with other children as well, and as a result, they were incarcerated.

The next letter was written by a thirteen year old girl to her father who had been sexually assaulting her for three years.

Dear Dad,

I know that you are mad at me for what I told the police and social worker, but you should never have touched me or Lynn in our private parts. You could have made me pregnant if I wasn't on the pill. I think that Lynn thinks that she is going to have a baby. Your baby dad. Your own daughter is going to have your baby. I hope that she gets an abortion.

I want you to know that I almost killed myself three different times. The first time was when you made me suck your penis. I went outside and took a gun from your shed, and I was going to shoot myself, but I wasn't able to find any bullets. The next time I took all the pills in your bathroom. Do you remember when I was in the hospital for five days? I took them because you had intercourse with me. Do you remember telling me in the hospital that if I told anyone why I took the pills that you would make sure that I would never see mom again. Do you remember that? Well I do and I don't see mom anymore because she thinks that I am lying about what you did to me. The other time I tried to kill myself was when I was on drugs. I became an alcoholic and a drug addict because I couldn't deal with what it was that you were doing to me. Mom doesn't believe me and she doesn't believe Lynn either. I hope that you and mom will be happy together without us. I know that I will, because I know that you will never be able to touch me ever again. I will pray for you and mom.

Your daughter,
Sandra

Sandra initially felt guilty because she spoke to the police and social worker about her sexual abuse. She disclosed the situation when she learned that her sister, Lynn, was also being sexually assaulted by her father. Both Lynn and Sandra were on birth control at the age of 13 and 14 years. Sandra had attempted suicide on three different occasions. She explained that the more she realized and accepted the fact that her father was touching her sexually, the less she was able to deal with it. The way out, she thought, that would allow the family to stay together, was to commit suicide. She decided after her three suicide attempts to explain to her mother what had occurred. (She found out later that her father had already prepared her mother for hearing "all sorts of strange things" from Sandra.)

Upon hearing Sandra's disclosure, her mother, for her own reasons, decided to support her husband. As a result of this, Sandra was removed from the home and withdrew the allegations from the authorities. Lynn was also removed from the home, but the two girls were separated and resided in separate foster homes.

The anger and alienation the victim feels is directed not only towards the offender. Victims often feel abandoned by their mothers to the control of their abusive fathers, and the letter below expresses these feelings clearly. It was written by a seventeen year old girl to her mother.

Dear Mom,
I am supposed to write you a letter and tell you how I felt about you when dad was sexually assaulting me. When dad first started touching me I was a little scared of you because I didn't know if what he was doing to me was right or not. It seems that I told you about a hundred times that he was touching me, but you seemed to never listen to me. I don't blame you any more for not stopping him, but I still don't know why you didn't do something about it. I'm confused because I don't know if you really knew about it or not. One time when dad tried to have intercourse with me and I tried to tell you about it, you said that you didn't have time to talk to me. You should have known that I was hurting inside, but you went bowling instead, I think.
I was asked to tell you about the time that I ran away from home when I went to stay at Aunt Cathy's house. I really wanted to hurt you because you never wanted to spend time with me. I think that this was about the time that you started to feel jealous about me and dad. I didn't like what dad was doing to me, but you made me feel like I was to blame, because you wouldn't talk to me. I felt like I needed to get back at you for not stopping him, and I hated him so much for what he was doing to me. I felt like you really rejected me because you kept pushing me away from you. Sometimes I felt that you were even pushing me towards dad. I know that that sounds really stupid but that's how I really felt. When you made comments about dad and I spending time together I thought you knew what dad was doing to me and that you didn't care. I thought dad was the only one back then who really loved me. When he started touching me I felt cared for and glad that he took some interest in me. You never seemed to do that. I really think now that all of us have a lot of things to work out, and I hope that we can get back together again in the near future.
Until I see you later,
Vicky

In her own mind, Vicky had provided numerous clues to her mother about the sexual abuse. She became angered and frustrated because she believed her mother was not responding to her pleas for help. Vicky's mother, although she was suspicious about the relationship between her husband and daughter, did not realize that incest was the problem.

Through treatment, these individuals were able to resolve

their problems, and create a happy family life together.

As I have tried to emphasize throughout this book, all the members of the incestuous family experience pain and lo self-esteem as a result of their own experiences growing up, and because of the dysfunctional relationships they share with each other. This letter from a non-offending mother to her daughter reveals these feelings, and at the same time indicates the growth of much healthier attitudes towards herself and her family as she progresses through the therapeutic process.

Dear Angie,

I hope that in this letter to you that I can set your mind at rest. That I don't hold you responsible for what your dad did. When the sexual abuse was going on I knew that something was not quite right in our family, but I did not ever think that it was this. I know that your father was attracted to you, and that sometimes I think that I felt a little jealous towards you for what I thought, at that time, you were doing. It seems like at times there was another woman living in the same house as me and we were both fighting over the same man. I know that that probably sounds really stupid to you, but it's true. I don't think that you really knew what was happening to you, but I sometimes question why you didn't stop it, at times why you didn't tell me about it. I guess you probably didn't think that I would believe you or that I would understand. I have come to understand a lot about why the sexual abuse happened in our family and even though I am not involved in the sexual part, I feel that I cared for myself more than I cared for looking after my children. In looking back I think I looked after your father more than I ever did myself or you. I know that I am going to be different now and I realize I am someone important and I don't need to have your father around anymore if I don't want him, but if your father can prove himself to me and you, then I will consider being with him, but not until that time. When I am able and willing to take care of myself, then I think I can be the person and the parent that I want and should be to you. I love you and am very proud of you.

Love Mom

Offenders too, experience a great deal of emotional anguish and regret for what they have done as they begin to strip away the defenses that have allowed them to escape responsibility for their actions. The following two letters were written near the beginning of the therapeutic process by offenders to their victims.

Dear My Little Karen,

Karen I am so sorry for hurting you like I did. I didn't mean to

---

hurt you and I hope that you will find it in your heart to some day forgive me for this. I was at the hospital each day that you were there, and I even stayed three nights. I would have stayed longer but the people at the hospital said I had to go home and get a good nights rest. I wasn't sleeping at all when I was there. I will make it up to you Karen once you are home. But before you come home I have to go to a rehabilitation center. You see I have a drinking problem and I want you to feel safe when you are at home with me. I hit you and touched you Karen when I was drunk and I never would have done that when I was sober. The drinking is not an excuse for me to do that to you, because I wanted to do that even when I wasn't drunk. But I think that the drinking made me think that it was o.k. I can't explain why I did some of those things to you, but after I get my problems straightened around then I will be able to understand them a bit better. I know that you are in a good home and that you will be well looked after there. I will write you lots of letters and when you are older I will read them to you. I have to go now, but please don't forget me. I won't ask you at this time to forgive me, not until I can prove myself to you. I love you Karen and I always will and I am oh so sorry for what I have done to you.

Your loving mother.

This letter was written by a single mother who had sexually assaulted her five year old daughter for just under two years. The child was placed in a foster home while the mother received treatment for her alcoholism and past sexual abuse.

The next letter was written by a male offender to his 16 year old daughter whom he had been sexually assaulting for 5 years.

Dear Angie,
When I look back on our family life I can recall so often feeling angry, confused and frustrated. Not knowing what to do and where to go. I spent most of my time feeling sorry for myself, and as a result of this took out my problems on you. I used to minimize what I had done to you and for that matter the rest of the family, until I started looking at myself and realized that I was taking the problems out that I had on all of you. When I used to touch you sexually, I can only recall being so angry at your mother and accused her of forcing me to do what I did. In saying this to you now, I am not trying to blame your mother, but just to tell you the type of thoughts that I had and the way that I justified it. The only person who is responsible for what I did to you Angie, is me. Definitely not you, and definitely not your mother and definitely no-one else. I only wish that you never had to face or feel this torment and pain that was created in you by me. I realize at times that you

were pretty protective of your mom, and for that matter of your brothers and sisters as well. You may not understand this but I'm pretty much a coward. I used to make you guys think that I was tough, so I would yell a lot and scream and throw things. I realized then, that that made you guys feel scared, and as a result of you being scared, I got my way. I'm learning now, not to have to do that and that I don't have to run from what I think and feel inside me anymore. It's going to take some time, but I will do whatever I possibly can to help you to understand. At first when I was separated from the family I thought everybody was doing things against me. I didn't even sit down for one moment to pay attention to what it was that I had done to you guys and how you guys must be feeling. Separating from you guys was probably the best thing for you and also for me, because it gave you time to begin to get your lives together without the threat of me being there and also it allowed me or really put me into a position of having to face my problems without running. I know that it's coming up pretty soon that we will be sitting down together and talking about this. I will do my best to help you understand. Right now, I'm doing my best to help me understand so that I can change my ways.

Love Dad.

In choosing to face his problems and take responsibility for his actions, this man successfully resolved the problems which lead to his sexually abusive behavior.

I'd like to close off this chapter with two rather lengthy letters which reflect the positive results that therapy can have on the individuals in incestuous families.

The first is from a 16 year old incest victim in the middle of the treatment process. Her letter reveals the horror of most of her life before disclosure, and her growing sense of optimism for the future, as all the members of her family tackle their problems and begin to resolve them.

A Letter to the World
from an Incest Victim

"I have existed on this earth for sixteen years now, however, I have only lived here since I was seven. Some of you know me as a careless person who really doesn't give a damn, others of you refuse to know me at all. If you took the time to talk to me and to show me you are interested in me, I might open up and share some things with you. However, these things I'm sure are things that you do not want to hear.

When I was just growing up, I think around four or five or so, I remember my mother and father constantly fighting. My dad was an alcoholic and I can remember at times him beating my mom up. My mom was really afraid of him and I realize now she tried to do her best, but back then she ran from him with terror. My memories of those years are kind of scary but not nearly as scary as living them because I was never sure from one minute to the other what that moment might bring.

My father started sexually assaulting me when I was around six. I wasn't sure what was going on, but I believed within myself that what he was doing was wrong and looking back now I realize that at six years old I wasn't very able to go to my mother or to my father or anyone else for that matter and talk to them about what was occurring. You see, I realized at six years old that no one would believe a six year old child when it comes to her word over an adult. Especially her parent. I realized back then that if I explained to my mother what was occurring, she would be placed in a position of having to support me over my father and I knew that she wasn't strong enough to do that.

In looking back now I realize that I used to parent my mother a lot more than she parented me. I realize now that I made a conscious decision, however, it didn't seem so conscious back then to keep the secret between my father and I. Before he started touching me I felt kind of like trash and scum of the earth anyways and didn't know whether or not I belonged to this family or not and through his touching me, it seemed to reinforce the fact that these thoughts and feelings were true.

As I am getting older I can remember hearing from people that children tend to play sides against their parents. In my upbringing, it was kind of opposite to that, my parents tended to play sides against me. I can remember so many times when my father would give me things and do things for me and at the same time criticize and run down my mother. He would tell me that she didn't love me and that she hated me and wanted to get rid of me. I felt so bad and so lost at times when he told me that, that I just didn't know what to do. It seems obvious now that my father knew what to do, because it was usually during those times that he would come and sexually assault me and tell me that he loved me and that he would never let anything bad happen to me. I had such a strong need to believe him that I accepted what he was doing to me and blocked every question of the incident out of my mind.

As I started getting older my mom really began to see the relationship between my father and I growing. It was fake, however, on both my father and my part because we knew it was just a game. A game I tried many times to get out of. I can remember on at least four or five different occasions going to my mother and telling her that I had something to discuss with her that was really important. She never ever took the time to listen to me. One day, I remember telling her that your husband is having sex with me, her response to that was, well I hope you enjoy it because he never has sex with me. When I heard this I thought that she was pushing me towards him and I felt angry and resentful. I realize now that my mother really didn't push me towards my father except at six, seven and eight years old, I really couldn't tell the difference.

When I was around nine and a half years old, my mom and dad went to visit some family in the United States and left me at my aunt's house. I didn't mind that too much, however, that was before I went there. You see, when I was there my uncle, like my father, also sexually assaulted me. I didn't view it as sexual assault back then, I viewed it as something I deserved because my uncle used to call me trash, and slut and he said he wanted to teach me a lesson. I won't go into detail as to what he did to me because your first question would probably be, why didn't I run or scream. Well, I didn't run or scream out loud but inside my head I screamed louder than anything you've ever heard. When my mom and dad came to pick me up, the first thing they asked my relatives were, how much trouble did I cause them. You see, I've been known to swear, mouth people off, and do drugs. My parents assumed, of course, that I would have done these things here as well and of course, I didn't. You see, or maybe you don't, but the only way that I knew how to deal with the fact that these things were occurring to me was to run. I couldn't physically run, so whenever I got stoned or drunk it seemed to ease the pain a little. That was until I woke up.

My father and my uncle stopped sexually assaulting me just before my sixteenth birthday. He promised many times before that to never touch me again but he always did. I wanted so much to believe him that he would never touch me again, that I felt sorry for him. I knew he had a problem and I didn't know how to help him. My father finally stopped touching me only after I physically ran away and lived with my boyfriend, who I might add, also did what he wanted with me both physically and sexually. I grew up in a home where people were treated like trash and I expected when I found somebody that I wanted to live with, he would obviously treat me like trash.

I didn't realize it then but I do now that I used to attract guys who had a need to hurt people, because back then I had a need to be hurt because that was the only way that I could prove that I was something. The pain was so real for me that it constantly reminded me of my nightmare. When I finally told my mom about what my dad was doing to me, she immediately called me a liar plus she called me every other thing she could think of. I realize now that she had a need to deny it because she too was a past victim of sexual abuse and she never dealt with it in her life until now.

I should probably add also that my father, sister and brother were also sexually assaulted when they were children. That by no means means that my father is justified in touching me but to me it means that he probably felt as much pain as I did. So many times when I was growing up I wanted to die, and on two different occasions, tried it. I began to feel that the only way to get rid of the pain was to get rid of the person. Thank God I failed at trying to commit suicide because now I realize that I am someone.

My mom and dad and I, actually our whole family, is going through treatment for the incest and sexual abuse that happened in our family. If I was to tell you that it was easy, I would be lying and I no longer lie. So the truth is, that it hurts, it hurts more than anything you can ever dream of but I am only a few months into the program and I realize now that this process is worth it because me and my mom and brother and sister and even my dad and uncle are really worth it. There is a reason those things occurred and if we punish the person without finding out the reason why it occurred, we gain nothing, and if I had any message to you at all, it would be this: for those of you who are victims of sexual abuse, remember that the person who is touching you has the ability to make you believe it's your fault. He or she has the ability to convince you that you are no good and that you're trash. For your sake if not for anyone elses, go to somebody you can trust and tell them, but better yet go to somebody who will also do something about it. Because if they promise you that it will stop, they're lying. It doesn't stop until you stop it.

For you mothers who hear for the first time or suspect that your daughter or son has been sexually assaulted, believe them. Right now more than anything else in their life they need you because tomorrow may come and they may not be there and you will feel guilty and bad and wish that you had done something sooner. Don't let that day pass, listen to them today, because when they come home stoned or drunk or tell you to F--- off, they are really telling you that they are hurting and they're scared and they don't know what to do. If you punish them for this, they will do it more. By this, I am not saying don't punish them, but I am saying get to know them, talk to them, listen to them, and believe them, because if you who are the biggest model in their life don't believe in them, neither will they believe in themselves.

For the fathers or the uncles, or any other person, whether they be male or female, who has sexually assaulted or has a desire to touch a child sexually, get help. You may try to convince yourself over and over again that you will never do it again, but ask yourself how many times you've said that, and how many times you've failed. I never thought that I could say this before but I realize now that I can, you are not animals, you are people who have problems and they need to be resolved. As long as you view yourself as an animal, you'll run and hide like an animal when they're scared. Stop running, take responsibility for what has happened and get help. I love my father very much and I realize now that he was not purposefully seeking to hurt me but has a strong need to feel important and wanted and cared for.

We can now have that loving family and as every week goes by it gets better and better. I would also like to say to you that it is not only girls who get sexually assaulted, it is also boys. My brother was sexually assaulted numerous times by both men and women. When my mother was young she sexually assaulted a boy that she babysat, I used to have thoughts of doing this also. I can only thank God that I never. I don't know what else to say to you other than, if you are in any trouble like this at all, phone someone, talk to someone who can and will help you end this nightmare.

Thank you, in dying memory. Kathy."

One final example, is a composite letter written by the offender, his wife, and abused daughter at the conclusion of treatment. It describes the evolution of a dysfunctional family into a healthy one, tracing the dynamics of the relationship between husband and wife from their first meeting, to the conclusion of family therapy.

The letter, which begins on the next page, is printed in the format of a dialogue in order to make clear which person wrote each section.

Our House

Bill: Because our children were not around when my wife and I first met, she and I will begin the story. I should probably start off and tell you that my name is Bill and my wife's name is Karen. The child that I sexually assaulted, her name is Linda and I have another daughter named Ann and a son named Terry. I met Karen when I was 21 years old and I had just finished serving a term in the military. After leaving the military I developed a drinking problem and was charged numerous times for fighting and disturbing the peace. Actually that's where I met Karen, in a bar, just before one of the times that I was arrested. I'm not really sure what attracted me to Karen, but I think it was the fact that she thought I was great. At least that's the impression she gave me. I learned later in my relationship with her that she didn't view me as being so great any more.

Karen: Actually when I met Bill I did view him as being somewhat of a show off, but he had something about him that drew me to him. Later on I think I learnt that I liked being around showy people because when they got attention then I got attention as well. Bill was always able to make me laugh and make me feel like I was important. I hated it when he was drinking though because he would scare me. Although at that time he would never hit me. I would usually think to myself that this would be the last time he will ever get drunk.

Bill: I remember promising Karen numerous times that I would stop drinking, and actually at the time I promised her I really wanted to stop. However I never ever did anything to try and stop and it seemed at the time to be an effective way of dealing with my problems. Anyways we were dating for about 6 months and I decided to ask her to marry me. I remember planning around trying to ask her to marry me and I thought the only way she would say yes is if I really impressed her. I thought of all sorts of things that I could do like having a plane write her name in the air, or ask her to marry me over the radio. But after I thought about that it took a lot of work to arrange and I thought maybe it was a stupid idea anyway. What I did do was one night when we were at a party I got everybody's attention and in front of our friends asked Karen if she would marry me.

Karen: When I first heard Bill say that he wanted to marry me at this party in front of all our friends, I was really shocked. The first thing that I thought was that we only really knew each other for a little while. I don't know if I really want to be married to a guy like that. Anyways I felt pressured but nonetheless still said

yes. Everybody around me seemed to be so excited that I kind of
joined in with the excitement and as a result we got married. Bill
and my mom and dad never really got along much together even
though my mom liked him more than my dad did. It seems now
when I look back that Bill was a lot like my dad. The same
problem with anger and the same problem with drinking. I was a
bit scared of my dad as well because of some of the things he used
to do to me.

Bill: I realized back then that I was a lot like Karen's father, but
there was no way that I was going to admit that, at least not then.
Sometimes Karen would make the comparison between me and
her dad and I would get really angry and tell her that I wasn't
like that. It's kind of funny now when I look back, because when I
got really angry at her that's exactly what her father used to do.
But when she heard my anger she would turn around and say,
"Ya, you're not like my dad." It didn't seem to make a whole lot of
sense back then.

Karen: Anyways Bill got a job as a truck driver and was away
from home a lot of the time. It seemed like whenever he came
home we were usually arguing, fighting, or he would go out with
his friends and get drunk. It seemed like I really didn't have a life
with him and it surely wasn't what I expected from a marriage.

Bill: I realize that Karen and I were drifting apart because I
wasn't home so often and so we thought we would have children.
Both of us were hoping that the children would draw us closer
together and make us a happy family. Well, we had children. The
first of which was Linda.

Karen: I remember when Linda was born I talked to Bill about
how he felt about having a girl first because he really wanted to
have a boy. He said that all families should have a boy first
because they have to be the strong ones and have to look after the
family after he is gone. Bill was really caught up on this 'men
have to do this, men have to do that' thing, back then and
sometimes it really drove me crazy.

Bill: I was annoyed at first when Linda was born and actually
even resented the fact that she was there. I really wanted to have a
boy because I thought most men really want to have boys, at least
at first. It seemed like I was really afraid to get close to Linda and
I would never pick her up or change her diapers. You know all
the types of things that women should do, (that's what I thought
back then). Though when she was about five or six years old it
seemed that she wanted to play around with me and do all sorts of
stuff. I really felt uncomfortable with this at first and I tended to

play a bit rough with her.

Karen: When I saw Bill play so rough with Linda I became pretty angry at him and I didn't hesitate at all to tell him so. He didn't seem to pay too much attention to what I was saying and I didn't know how to make him stop. It seemed that we were being pushed further and further apart and I didn't have any control over him and that really bothered me. I remember Bill would want me to come to bed at night and the first thing he would want to do was to have sex, especially if he just came home from trucking. I started withholding that from him because I thought there's no way he's going to be gone all this time and just walk back into the house and try and have sex with me. I wondered who he thought I was that I would let him do that. I was a bit suspicious that he was having sex while he was gone trucking, but I never did ask him. At least not then.

Bill: When Karen wouldn't give me sex, I became pretty frustrated with that and pretty angry, and I found myself for some reason drawing closer and closer to Linda. At least Linda was paying some attention to me. That was more than I could say that Karen was doing. When Linda was talking a lot more she was telling me that she loved me and cared for me and just made me feel good and for some reason I found myself being attracted to her. I remember once when we were wrestling around on the ground I put my hand or cupped it over her vagina area. It didn't seem to bother her and she didn't make any noises about it and she sure didn't tell me to stop. So I didn't think it bothered her. When I remember back now I also remember getting an erection and I was really scared that Karen would find out I did that.

Karen: I used to notice that when Bill and Linda were fooling around on the floor wrestling I was a bit resentful that they were having that kind of relationship, when the only thing that Bill wanted me for was to clean the house and to look after his every need. I don't know why but I started to become angry at Linda and resentful, actually quite jealous of the fact that they had that relationship. Something that I never had with Bill.

Linda: I can't remember the first time that my dad touched me but in talking to him he told me that he had cupped his hand over my vagina, I don't really recall that, but I do recall wrestling around with him and he would sometimes touch my breasts and maybe brush his leg or the back of his hand between my legs. I didn't really know what to think when he first did that, but I thought that if my dad was doing this, it must be o.k. It seems that at least he was paying some attention to me, when my mom never did. It seemed like my mom was really angry because my dad and

I had a good relationship, (or what seemed to be a good relationship at the time.)

Bill: As Linda started growing up I started to really become aware of the fact that she was starting to look like a woman. I realize now that she wasn't a woman at twelve years old, but she was starting to develop breasts, and I really became aroused when I looked at her. By this time the relationship between Linda and I at least sexually was quite often. I was probably touching her private parts almost every week. Sometimes more and sometimes even less. But usually once a week or so. By this time the relationship between Karen and I was almost non-existent except for the fighting and arguing that we did. My memory of that time really was one that I blamed her for everything that went wrong in my life, which seemed to justify, for me anyway, what I was doing to Linda. I did notice, however, that when Linda was around thirteen years old that she really didn't like what I was doing to her. But by that time I didn't know how to stop or didn't know how to deal with what was going on.

Karen: I remember that time as well, when Linda was around twelve or thirteen years old that the relationship between Bill and Linda was going from one of being really close to sometimes one of a lot of anger and distance. I didn't know what to make of it. They seemed a lot of times to even act like man and wife. I guess I dealt with it by keeping to myself and at times, when I was feeling really down, I saw myself sometimes turning to Linda as well. She almost seemed to be like a parent to me and would look after the family.

Linda: Like my mom and dad I also remember when I was thirteen years old. It was a pretty difficult time for me. It was around that time that I began to really realize that what my dad was doing to me was wrong. I didn't know how to stop it so I just kind of went along with it. I also realize that at times when my dad did that to me he gave me things as well, usually money. He would leave it sometimes on my dresser when he would leave the room. I'm so embarrassed to say this, but I remember once wanting some money so I started wrestling around with my dad, knowing darn well that he was going to touch my breasts and vagina when we were wrestling and I also knew that he would feel real guilty after he did it and usually put some money on my dresser. Well he did that and did put money on my dresser and I went out and had a good time that night, spending the money. It seemed after a while that it almost became a game between him and I. Neither of us knew how to stop it. When my sister, Ann and brother, Terry were born, they're twins, I was really scared that my dad was going to start touching them as well. I remember taking on the job of looking after them and for a time I really felt like I was their parent. The more I did for them it seemed the more they wanted and the more my mom and dad made me do for them. After a while it seemed like we could live without my mom in the house. She started doing all sorts of volunteer work and always playing bingo or something like that.

Bill: Once after I had intercourse with Linda, I think she was probably around fifteen years old, I felt so guilty about what I did, I told her to go and tell somebody so this could stop. In the back of my mind I was saying this because I really wanted her to tell somebody so it would stop, but I also knew that she would feel guilty knowing that I seemed so helpless with the situation. When I told that to Linda she started crying and gave me a hug and said it was o.k. I felt really terrible at that time and went out and got really drunk. That tended to be the way I dealt with things anyways. It seemed like whenever a problem happened I would get drunk or I would yell at Karen or at either Ann or Terry. Ann and Terry were pretty young then but I still seemed to be able to justify yelling at them.

Karen: Bill did do that a lot, yelling at them I mean. It seemed like whenever he was upset he would have to take his anger out on someone else. But it's even funny because even when he started to feel sad or hurt he would also get angry and take it out on other people. I didn't understand that until recently, but he really feared dealing with stuff like that. It's funny saying that now because I used to do the same thing, because after my daughter disclosed her sexual abuse I was also able to talk about mine. It seems like my daughter and I had a lot in common, but it also seemed like Bill and I had a lot in common as well.

Bill: When Linda finally disclosed to the police the first thing that I wanted to do was talk to Karen. I thought that if I could just get her to believe me that I didn't do it, we could easily make Linda look as a liar. Her mom always thought she was a liar and called her a slut and a tramp and a whore. So maybe we were able to blame it on that. Unfortunately, (or fortunately now) I wasn't able to find Karen and try to convince her of that. But the police found her first and talked to her. The police were able to make Karen believe that Linda was telling the truth and when I knew that Karen believed Linda I felt pretty scared and I admitted to part of what Linda was saying. At the time that we are writing this letter Linda is twenty-one years old and in her second year of nursing school. We decided as a conclusion to this letter that each of us would write a brief statement of kind of like what we think now. I'll go first.

I realize now that the reason I was attracted to Karen was

---

because she let me get away with everything. She didn't stick up for herself and she made me feel important. She was somebody that I was easily able to control and manipulate and make her do almost anything I wanted. I realize that the way I related to her and my family, was a way in which I was raised at home. I never felt love or caring and I can't remember the last time that my mom and dad told me that they love me. I was able to understand this and deal with this and get some help for myself and I'm very pleased to say that we are all living together now in a happy family.

Karen: I realize that when I met Bill he provided a very father-like image for me and was really a lot like my dad. My dad, by the way, sexually assaulted me when I was a child. I didn't realize it then but he and Bill had a lot in common. When I met Bill I really felt kind of trash-like and Bill was really able to reinforce that in me, but I was willing and able to accept that. I blamed Bill for that for a lot of years but realize now that it was my own doing. When the kids got older, especially Linda, I realize that I knew pretty much that Bill was touching her sexually. I found it very difficult back then to ever admit that. And even now I still feel a lot of guilt when I say it. I knew though that if I went to tell somebody about it, that Bill would probably end up leaving me or going to jail and I would have to live by myself, raising three children. I found it difficult raising the three children even knowing that Bill was around, even though he didn't seem to do anything to help. I realize that I played a lot of the same games in the family that Bill played, and probably for pretty much the same reasons. When we got into treatment it seemed that the hardest relationship to work out was the one between me and Linda, and not the one between Bill and Linda, which it seems like one would expect. Anyways, I'm really glad to say that all that has worked out now. Bill no longer drives a truck and he's home almost every evening. We seem to be happier now than we ever have.

Linda: I realize now that I am not to blame for what my dad did to me and I no longer resent my mom for not stopping it. I thought that back then she was kind of encouraging it, and pushing me to my dad. I found out later from her that in some ways she was but she said she wasn't really meaning for me to have sex with him. Her and I have been able to sort this whole thing out and we've got a real good relationship now. My dad and I get along really well, and I no longer have any fear that he is going to touch me sexually. I really despised him for what he was doing because it made me feel so dirty and cheap. When I finally disclosed to the police about what he did, I found it really, really hard to do because a couple of times when I was babysitting I got real curious with the kids I was looking after and fondled their private parts.

This made me feel real dirty and cheap, kind of like how I viewed my father, because I saw myself so much like him in that way, I thought that there was no way that I could tell anybody about what he did to me. I feared so strongly having to tell them what I did to those kids. Anyways that's all worked out now and I'm in nursing school and things are going pretty well. I still go and spend a lot of time at home and I'm really glad that the relationship between us is a real happy one. I really became scared when I thought my dad was going to start touching Ann and Terry, that I kind of felt that I had to protect them. It seemed like I was doing everything in the family anyways and protecting them just seemed like another thing that somebody should do. I realize now that the more I did that the more my mom and dad wanted me to start looking after everything. I think though that in looking back, because I was so insistent that I look after Ann and Terry, my dad didn't touch them. He says to me though, that the reason he never touched them was because they were so different than I was. He says that he was really scared that if he ever touched them they would tell somebody. I realize now that I wasn't that type of person. I mean an assertive person way back then.

My sister Ann and brother Terry don't have a whole lot to say because they are still pretty young. I can see the difference in them now because my dad stopped being so domineering and controlling in the family and my mom is starting to take some responsibility for herself. It seems like Ann and Terry are starting to open up and are starting to talk about how they feel and they never ever did before. All of us have changed in so many ways now, that I'm really glad to say that we are a happy family. It's nice to be able to go home and put my arms around my mom and dad and feel the love that we have for each other and not view them as enemies. Well so long from the Jones family. We hope that the information we have provided you with has helped.

Chapter 9
Responding to the Problem

(A Brief Overview)

The problem of incest and child sexual abuse tends to be self-perpetuating unless the cycle is broken by therapeutic intervention. This chapter gives a very brief description of the treatment method used by Martens & Associates.

Philosophy and Assumptions

As we have seen, incestuous families are composed of individuals caught up in an interrelated system of unhealthy, dysfunctional relationships, and everyone involved suffers from negative self-concept and low self esteem.

The parents, who lay the foundation for this system, often come from a background where incest or child sexual abuse has occurred within their own families; most have, themselves, been sexually assaulted. Unconsciously acting in the way they have been taught, they tend to enter into dysfunctional adult relationships which reflect and perpetuate the abuse they have suffered in the past. In so doing, they often shape their children into the next generation of offenders and/or victims.

In order to break this cycle, and successfully rehabilitate the individuals who make up the incestuous family, efforts are made to improve each individual's image of himself. A punitive approach to the problem serves only to intensify the negative self-image, thereby increasing the likelihood that the aggressive behavior will continue.

The foundation of our treatment model, therefore, is based on a humanistic philosophy; we make the following assumptions about people:

1. Human beings are basically good, and given the opportunity, they will strive towards that end.

2. Each individual is unique.

3. People have a personal responsibility for the choices they make and the consequences they entail.

4. People are capable of change and self-awareness which

leads to the ability to choose and change behavior.

5. Human beings are basically pro-social; they want to feel good about themselves, and have a need to relate to others in order to develop a sense of self.

6. The normal human tendency towards growth and self-actualization sometimes needs a little assistance.

The Treatment Process

Within this philosophical framework, our treatment approach first attends to the needs of the individual members of the incestuous family. Then we gradually bring together these individuals, who are in the process of healing and personal growth, for dyadic sessions (sessions with the therapist and one other family member), family therapy, and family reconstruction.

The process begins when incest or child sexual abuse is first disclosed by the victim, or the offender voluntarily seeks help, and lasts for approximately 18 months. The therapeutic approach is very similar for each person: victim, offender, non-offending parent(s) and siblings.

At the onset of treatment, the offender is usually removed from the family environment, either by court order or voluntarily. This is necessary both to identify and correct the problems dealing with roles within the family, and to ensure the safety of the child victim and other children in the home. And because incest tends to have its basis in issues pertaining to power and control over other people, it is extremely difficult to deal with these issues with the offender still residing in the home. Throughout the process, in cases where the offender has been charged with an offense, the courts monitor his progress.

The offender's absence also allows time for the child victim, her siblings and their mother (non-offending spouse), to begin working on their own dysfunctional relationships.

Prior to commencing with therapy, all individuals go through a series of assessments to determine the types of services they require and the methods through which those services should be delivered.

Individual Therapy

The therapeutic process begins with individual therapy for each member of the family. We focus on four main areas: the physical self, emotional self, psychological self, and spiritual self.

If the individual's physical self is suffering from severe headaches, stomach problems or back pain, he/she is often referred to doctors, nutritionists, chiropractors or others trained to treat these problems. We need to understand whether the person's pain is caused by emotional problems, or by a physical agent.

In treating the emotional self, we help individuals to understand feelings that tend to be very strongly related to their past experiences. We help them to understand why they feel what they do, why they interpret things the way they do, and how these interpretations express themselves through their actions. Often through treating the emotional self, headaches or other physical symptoms go away.

In the area of the psychological self, we deal with what people think and why they view things the way they do. Here too, the past strongly shapes attitudes. We help people to make a transition between the psychological and emotional selves, enabling them to differentiate between what they think and what they feel.

In addressing the spiritual self, which has a great impact on the other aspects of the self, individuals are encouraged to examine and evaluate their goals and direction in life, to review what they believe in terms of morals, values and ethics, and why they believe it. Pastors, ministers or other clergy may be drawn on for assistance.

In all cases, the goals of individual therapy are to raise the self-esteem and improve the self-concept of the people involved, and to assist them in expressing thoughts and feelings. In addition, specific treatment goals are pursued for each person.

The victim is helped to understand why she was chosen by the offender to be sexually assaulted, why the abuse continued, and why she is not responsible for it. She is helped to replace angry self-abusive behaviors such as running away, alcohol or drug abuse, and violence with more positive avenues of expression such as art therapy, enabling her to express, understand, and resolve conflicts of the past. The pictures produced are a potent vehicle to help alleviate nightmares, fears and phobias in children, adolescents and adults.

Individual therapy with siblings of the victim is very similar to that for victims. Although the siblings may not have been sexually touched, they can be affected by the offender's abusive power and control, and process of manipulation and coercion just as much as the child who was assaulted. Siblings, therefore, have the same issues to deal with as victims: developing trust and self-esteem, gaining a sense of self-identity, dealing with denial, and learning self-control.

The non-offending parent, who may have chosen to ignore or deny the abuse occurring within her family, is encouraged through treatment to verbalize the reality of the sexual abuse and hear the story from the child victim and the offender. She is also helped to deal with her own past history of abuse, identify unreasonable expectations, practise the setting of limits and improve body awareness. Other issues addressed are feelings of failure, and depression. She is also provided with support through the legal justice system.

The offender, too, often denies that incest has occurred, and may comply with the therapy solely in order to satisfy a court order. When treatment begins, however, and he is confronted by the therapist and (eventually) other offenders, "going along for the ride" becomes impossible. Individual therapy sessions for the offender usually occur once or twice a week for one to three hours.

Through treatment, he comes to realize that he alone is responsible for the sexual act occurring. He is helped to face and share his own past history of abuse, to increase his tolerance of frustration and improve the way he deals with it. He is also helped to increase his awareness of his feelings, and his ability to communicate these to others in a healthy manner. In addition he learns to develop impulse control and empathic ability, and to manage sexual and aggressive drives.

Group Therapy

At approximately the same time that the individual therapy begins with the members of an incestuous family, each person also engages in group therapy with other people who share their circumstances: victims join a victims' group, offenders meet with other offenders, etc. Groups meet once a week for three to six hours.

For the child victim, meeting in group therapy with others who have been sexually victimized helps her to realize that she is not alone, that others have experienced many of the same feelings and thoughts that she has, and that the trauma of abuse can be effectively dealt with. The support of other victims also helps her to deal with the issues she faces in individual therapy.

Meanwhile, offenders meet and discuss personal issues with others who have committed similar offenses. They too, with the support of the group, confront the same issues they face in individual therapy. The group provides them with a safe place to practise expressing feelings, and develop empathy for others.

Similarly, in their groups, non-offending spouses and siblings receive support to face the issues they must deal with in order to rebuild their families on a healthy foundation.

Reconstructing the Family

For the first three or four months of treating the incestuous family, the offender is segregated from the rest of the family. During this time, the child victim meets with her mother and sibling(s) in dyadic sessions with the therapist. This provides a means for them to work on and resolve issues that have been created among themselves, such as feelings of jealousy, resentment and anger.

After three or four months of individual and group therapy, the offender first begins his reintegration with the family through dyadic sessions with the sibling(s) of his victim. In these, he confronts the abusive and manipulative way he has exercised power over them.

At about the same time, or slightly later depending on the readiness of both people, he meets with his child victim for the first time in the therapist's office. In this session he tells the victim why he sexually assaulted her and what he believed he gained from it. He accepts full and complete responsibility for the sexual acts and for the manipulative coercive manner in which he set up the child to be abused. In the same session, the child explains her thoughts and feelings to the offender so that he can understand and feel the damage he has done to her. This encounter begins to bring home to the offender the reality of what he has done.

If this session is beneficial to both the child victim and the offender, they may continue to meet, under the supervision of the therapist, about once every two weeks, until their involvement in treatment needs to become more regular. Around the sixth or seventh month, they meet with the therapist on a weekly basis.

Meanwhile, the offender begins couple therapy with his spouse. During this process they discuss such issues as why they got married, the quality of their marriage, and what the future holds for them as a couple.

At about the eighth month of therapy, the offender makes a transition in treatment from thinking and believing that he is responsible for the sexual act, to actually feeling his own pain and the pain of his victim. When this occurs, a night-and-day transformation takes place in the way he deals with anger, frustration, hostility, happiness, sadness, responsibility and accountability.

At approximately the eleventh month, if the family reconstruction is progressing well and all members of the family agree, the offender goes home for the first time, for a one to four hour visit with a clear agenda. A scrupulous review of the visit is completed by the therapist and family members, and if the situation appears beneficial for all, home visits continue and increase over time. Family therapy commences at about this same time. By the twelfth or thirteenth month of treatment, the offender may be home on a full time basis, while continuing with his individual, couple and family therapy.

Conclusion

The treatment process is lengthy and demanding, and because individuals are so different, it is impossible to gage how each person will do in treatment as a whole. For some families, from the point of disclosure through to the completion of treatment, the process is relatively smooth and free of legal or therapeutic problems.

For others, it can be very different. The child may meet with anger, frustration or rejection on disclosing, and refuse treatment and even retract the initial allegations. The offender may sincerely want treatment to deal with his problems, but receive a jail term instead.

These problems are unfortunate, but they do sometimes occur. It would be a mistake to assume that immediately following disclosure, a dramatic improvement is made in the quality of life of an incestuous family. However, hundreds of individuals have gone through the therapeutic process and turned their lives around. These people are now living very healthy, productive, harmonious lives that they once thought would never occur.

After treatment has been completed, the offenders and their families are followed-up for approximately five years in order to assess how well they are coping, and to see whether or not incest or sexual assault occurs again. To this date, as far as we know, none of the offenders who have completed treatment through our program have committed incest or child sexual abuse again. By contrast, the reoccurrence rate for offenders jailed without treatment is often very high.

(We will describe our therapeutic process in much greater detail in a future publication from Martens & Associates.)

Chapter 10
Training Care Givers
to Assist Others

Developing an awareness of the signs and symptoms of incest and child sexual abuse is an ever growing concern for anyone who cares about the welfare of children. To this end, agencies and communities are providing training to people working in other human service occupations. For example, *Signs and Symptoms* workshops are often given to people involved in child welfare or drug and alcohol counselling.

This growth in awareness of the problem offers great promise that more cases of abuse will be uncovered, and that the individuals involved will be helped towards a healthier, happier life.

However, the offering of *Signs and Symptoms* workshops must be approached with caution and sensitivity. The workshops should be specific and central to the task that the care giver has in his or her place of employment. It is quite unrealistic to assume that one individual care giver can provide a vast array of therapy services ranging from drug and alcohol treatment, wife battering treatment, family counselling, and incest and child sexual abuse treatment.

The most important consideration in offering such workshops, however, lies in paying attention to the emotional readiness of the individuals in attendance, to handle information dealing with incest and child sexual abuse. Our experience has shown us that many of the people attending these workshops have a multitude of unresolved issues in their own lives; many are, themselves, the victims of past sexual abuse.

Our experience has also been that a *Signs and Symptoms* workshop can provide an environment in which untreated victims will acknowledge and disclose their abuse for the first time. It is imperative, therefore, that great sensitivity be shown to the emotional needs of these people, when such workshops are offered. Plans for dealing with new disclosures of sexual abuse by people attending the workshops should be in place before the workshops are held.

It is also essential, that these "care givers/victims" resolve their own issues **before** attempting to assist others. Otherwise, unresolved issues surrounding their own abuse, will prevent them from working objectively and effectively with families which need their help. *(Maggie Hodgson deals with this subject as it relates to Native care givers, in much more detail in Chapter 12.)*

Care givers who are victims of abuse, and have never worked through their trauma to the point of resolution, **cannot** effectively assist others to resolve sexual abuse issues. Their confusion about their own abuse often blocks their ability to be empathic, objective and caring towards all members of an incestuous family. Consequently, the results of untreated care givers/victims working with incestuous families, are likely to be devastating not only for themselves, but also for the families they are working with.

For example, untreated care givers/victims may find themselves reacting very inappropriately when dealing with offenders. Reactions can range from projecting a strong sense of rage, anger and frustration, to responding in an extremely passive or submissive manner. Neither reaction is good for the care giver, or for the individuals they are working with. Therefore, care givers/victims must be helped to address issues in their own lives, prior to attempting to assist others.

Another important consideration when developing workshops, seminars and lectures on this subject, is to build in a component which addresses culture and spirituality. These elements are often key to the development of individuals, and become the basis of their being. Frequently, the clients we deal with in treatment are afraid of these issues, feeling a sense of non-being, confusion and embarrassment when they are raised. Therefore, it is essential that care givers working with such individuals have their own spiritual and cultural houses in order.

In spite of the complexity of incest and child sexual abuse issues, and the repercussions involved with even creating greater awareness of them, addressing the issues offers our only hope of their resolution.

The problem has always been with us, but in the past it has been hidden by secrecy. As incest and child sexual abuse issues come out of the closet, and more human services practitioners become skilled in assisting the families affected, we can look forward to this problem being less pervasive in the future, than it has been in the past.

Chapter 11

The Roots of the Problem in Native Communities
by Brenda Daily

Introduction

In order to understand some of the present day factors which have impact on Native families which are experiencing family violence and child abuse, it is helpful to have some knowledge of the historical context from which Native people have emerged.

This chapter gives a brief overview of significant historical forces which have influenced Native families and culture, and the differing kinds of legal status held by Native people. It also deals with elements unique to Native experience (eg. the role of "elders", Native spirituality), and with substance abuse, which are important factors in helping Native families deal with problems of abuse.

Historical Influences on Native Culture

First Contact

Just as there were many Indian nations co-existing on the North American continent at the point of European contact, there were also many cultures. Culture (ie. the customary beliefs, social norms and material traits of a racial, religious or social group) is not a fixed entity; it is a moving, transforming dynamic force which is impacted by time and the introduction of new concepts and beliefs.

European cultures contained many beliefs and values that differed from Native concepts. Not the least of these were ideas about family, starting with the basic understanding of what family was. Because Europeans became the dominant race on the North American continent, they were able to impose their values and beliefs onto Native peoples.

It is important for us to acknowledge that this is still affecting Native families and the individuals within those units. Government policy regarding Native people affects the decisions that can be made for and by Native people regarding problem *solving with troubled families.*

The Fur Trade

In the 1700's, Europeans established the fur trade and introduced the idea of private property. The fur traders would deal only with men who represented heads of families. Thus the nuclear family began to replace extended family units and women began to lose their status. Pressures on Native families came not only from the fur trade itself, but also from church missions which grew up simultaneously with it. Missionaries began to convert Natives from "pagan" beliefs to Christianity, and taught different ideas and values about family. For example, the church encouraged the use of corporal punishment by men to "discipline" their women and children. (It is recorded that church missionaries were appalled by the lenient way in which Indian people dealt with their children, and by the freedom of Indian women.)

During the fur trade years, Native people comprised the backbone of the labour force. Women were a part of this economic and social order because they possessed viable skills necessary to sustain the trade.

With the decline of the fur trade and the influx of European settlers, Native people were no longer needed as a labour force; only the land they lived on was desired.

Disease, and Famine

New ideas about family and property, however, were not the only European influences which eroded Native concepts of family. Another devastating influence was disease. Smallpox became a scourge among Natives who had no immunity to it. It completely destroyed entire nations including the Mandan, who disappeared with the epidemic of 1820. It is estimated that the last great smallpox epidemic in 1870 wiped out one half to two thirds of the western Native population.

Along with disease, came famine, as the Plains buffalo herds began to vanish because they were hunted to near extinction. To the disease and famine ridden Natives, the promise of food and medicine was one of the greatest bargaining tools of the treaty negotiations.

The Treaty Process and Legal Status of Native People

In 1870, the Dominion of Canada acquired for the sum of three hundred thousand pounds, the territory owned by the Hudson Bay Company which comprised all the western region draining into the Hudson Bay. Between 1871 and 1879, eight major treaties were signed between the crown and Native people. These treaties secured lands from Ontario to Alberta.

After the Native people's land was secured via the treaty process and the Native population was removed from the mainstream society onto reserves, the Indian Act (1925-1951) banned political organizing including many traditional gatherings such as Potlaches on the West Coast and Sundances on the Plains.

As a result of historical factors, there are several different divisions of Native people recognized legally within the Canadian Constitution:

Status Indians are individuals registered under the Indian Act. They have rights to certain benefits including residence on reserves, special federal programs and tax exemptions.

Metis are individuals of mixed blood (Half-breeds.) The word originally applied to people of French/Indian ancestry but now includes anyone with mixed European and Indian ancestry. Metis, as a group, had no treaties and were not registered under the Indian Act. Some Metis did register during the signing of treaties and became recognized as status Indians. Metis as a group had their aboriginal rights recognized in the Manitoba Act of 1870.

The Northwest Resistance marked the end of the Metis' right to their land in Saskatchewan in 1885. In Alberta only, the province granted Metis land via the Metis Settlements. This land is subject to a ninety-nine year lease; the government never gives up ownership.

Inuit, Inuvialiut are Native people living in the far North. They had no significant treaties, no reserves, and do not come under the terms of the Indian Act.

Non-status Indians are Indians who do not have registered status; they are Native people not recognized by the Constitution. These people lost their status in many ways: Status Indian women lost their status if they married a white, non-status Indian or Metis man*; some Indians were paid to give up their status; others lost status when they went to war to fight for their country; others were not present at the original treaty signings; (This included tribes who had refused conversion to Christianity prior to treaty signing. These tribes were not actively solicited by Treaty negotiators who were often missionaries.)

**Recent amendments to Bill C-31 have granted status back to women (and their children) who lost status because of marrying non-status men.*

The Whiskey Trade

Alcohol was another devastating influence on Native societies. Illegal whiskey traders created great pressures on the family through their selling of "firewater". (One old recipe consisted of three gallons of water mixed with one gallon of alcohol; one pound of chewing tobacco; one pound of tea for color; ginger and a handful of red peppers.)

Assimilation and Residential Schools *

Assimilation was government policy which determined that over time, Native people would be taught the values and skills of the dominant society in order to "civilize" them. The common belief was that eventually Natives would disappear as a distinct cultural and political group, that they would willingly give up Status once they understood the difference in lifestyles and values.

The policy was aimed at the young and carried out in the context of religion and education; the mandate for implementing it was given to the missionaries. To achieve the maximum effect, children were removed at the earliest age, and to the largest degree possible, from the influences of their own culture, ie. their homes, and often their communities.

Beginning in 1830, mission schools were established. In the latter part of the 1880's industrial schools which taught agriculture and homemaking skills were established, followed in the early years of the twentieth century, by residential schools. Most of these operated into the 1960's, with the result that many Indian children spent their entire childhood living away from their families, often hundreds of miles from the reserve. They saw their families of origin only once or twice a year.

In the residential schools, Indian children were taught English or French. Many children were punished if they spoke their language or practiced traditional customs including singing Native songs. Native spirituality was replaced by Christianity. Children were often told that old spiritual ways were evil and the work of the devil.

Separation of the children culturally and geographically from parents and their way of life had a drastic impact on almost all Indian families. The structure, cohesion and quality of family life suffered. Old productive skills tied to the land were lost. Parenting skills diminished as succeeding generations became more and more institutionalized and experienced little nurturing. Low self-esteem and self-concept problems arose as children were taught that their own culture was inferior and uncivilized, even "savage."

The policy of not establishing ordinary services such as

*Acknowledgement given to information provided by Alberta Social Services Training Resources
110   document entitled Canada's Native People.

education on the reserves resulted in communities that could not support their own members. Consequently, reserves became caught between two worlds: on the one hand they remained outside modern social and economic development, and on the other, they had little access to traditional patterns.

The Child Welfare System *

After World War II residential schools were phased out slowly to be replaced by the Child Welfare system which began policies of intervention to remove children from dysfunctional family systems. Many children were taken into care and placed far from their families, often in non-Native environments. This system culminated in the 1960's with an apprehension rate so high that some reserves lost nearly a generation of children to child welfare authorities.

Recent figures show that Indian children are placed in care at four and one-half times the rate for all children in Canada. In comparison to .96% of all children in Canada, 4.6% of all Status Indian children age nineteen and under are in care. (Johnson 1983) Seventy-five percent of Indian children who are adopted go to non-Native homes.

Culture, Heritage and Tradition

Confusion about culture, heritage and tradition is a major issue for many Native people. Non-Natives may also become confused and may fall into stereotyped perceptions of Native people. It is often helpful for people to define *culture* as "the way we live now" and *heritage (or tradition)* as "the way our ancestors lived."

Many Native individuals are in an active process of trying to regain traditions and heritage that were lost. Incorporating nineteenth century tribal traditions into a twentieth century, often urban environment frequently leads many Native people into what's described as an "identity crisis", a state of severe anxiety.

The Native Concept of "Elder"

Often in Native country, someone seeking solutions to problems will be told: "Go see an Elder." In order to do this we need to clarify who an "Elder" is. Some definitions are as follows:

- A person who has grown expert at living life. An individual who has lived well and is regarded with respect. This person is often seen as a resource in regard to his/her particular wisdom and expertise and can be sought out for

---

Acknowledgement given to information provided by Alberta Social Services Training Resources document entitled Canada's Native People.

111

advice and counsel- eg. a good hunter, hide preparer, fisherman, bead worker, healer, etc. This area of expertise was indicative of the functional role the person had played within the community circle.

• Individuals who are Pipe Holders or Spiritual Leaders. These people can be approached for spiritual or cultural training, consulted for "healing", or for leading ceremonies such as sweat lodges. There is a specific manner, including integral steps, involved in approaching a Pipe Holder. Anyone wishing their service or counsel should find out what these steps are in order to be perceived or understood to be behaving "respectfully."

• Anyone older than yourself, as in "respect your Elders."

• A senior citizen, a person over 65 who has special financial and legal status under Canadian Law. They are given a monthly pension and receive grants and benefits.

As we can see, in different Native communities, the word "Elder" means different things to different people. There are several reasons for this diversity of definition.

In some cases, assimilation into the White dominant society separated Native people from their cultural values, beliefs, roles and language.

Linguistic differences also account for variations in meaning. Native languages contain words which describe roles and philosophical ideas which are not found in English. The description of a concept, therefore, does not always translate from one language to the other.

In other cases, the hierarchical structure of Christian religious and church systems define only some individuals, eg. Priest, Bishop, Minister, Pope, Deacon, etc, as a spiritual leader or expert. This concept of "spiritual order" is sometimes projected onto Native spirituality which was originally highly individualized and egalitarian. A projection of hierarchical order can occur when a Native person who was raised within Christian doctrine reverts to or reclaims Native cultural/spiritual beliefs.

Another point which could cause confusion is that a basic component of admirable Native character is humility. Therefore, an "Elder" will often not claim to be one.

No one definition is necessarily right or wrong; however, the differences point to a need for dialogue to clarify understanding and acceptance of individual opinion. It is important, therefore, to remind oneself that attitudes and values come from an enormous diversity in individual Native experience. The dialogue around cultural values and definitions is often highly charged and emotional because it stems from experiences which were sometimes painful.

Native Spirituality

There is often great diversity in the spiritual beliefs of the members of a single family. In examining the issue, it can be helpful to clarify who believes what. Some Native individuals follow the traditional path. Others no longer understand, accept or desire traditional concepts or beliefs. The latter have adopted and are satisfied with the definitions of the non-Native world. They may range from being practicing Catholics to Born Again Christian fundamentalists.

In some cases, differing spiritual beliefs within a family may be an area of high tension and emotional pain.

Characteristics of Natives in Incestuous Families

Negative Self Image

The general problem of low self-esteem and negative self-image among all the members of incestuous families is compounded among Native people by a variety of factors. For example, the self-image of one or both parents has probably been affected by racial stereotyping and/or prejudice. In addition, many Natives have experienced some form of institutionalization such as residential school, foster care, or imprisonment. These experiences have affected their problem-solving abilities, parenting skills, and ability to trust and form intimate relationships.

Native adults are also usually handicapped by low levels of formal education (only 18% graduate from high school) and, in cases where English is their second language, by language difficulties as well. All of these factors increase their sense of isolation and negative image of themselves.

Native male offenders often have subscribed to a very "macho" image of male sexuality. This may be an attempt, at least in part, to compensate for feelings of inferiority. The Native male may feel that his sense of manhood is threatened by a precarious employment status, economic insecurity, and a sense of powerlessness in a white male dominant society. As a result, he may react in his own home by wanting to hold a superior position, to be in control and have his needs met, and by blaming others for what he is doing.

In addition, some Native males have had their sense of sexual identity shaped by time spent in jails or other institutions where sex and power were tied together. In such environments, where manhood is equated with toughness, they have needed to suppress many of their feelings. They may have been assaulted or coerced into sexual activity by the promise of status or physical survival. Later, they may feel very ashamed of these activities and worry that they are gay.

Native people are also often affected by high stress linked to low income, housing problems, and crises within the family such as deaths. All of this may be complicated by other forms of abuse and violence occurring at the same time. There is a high probability that one or more family members has a problem with drugs or alcohol, and that one or both parents grew up in homes where there were alcohol-related problems.

Sexual Innocence

Native women who were raised in convents or residential schools often have little or no knowledge about sexuality. Sometimes they have been taught very distorted concepts. They do not have the experience of sexuality being discussed in the open. Indeed, the whole topic of sexuality may be acutely embarrassing, and the subject avoided. Some view all sex as painful or disgusting, and cannot distinguish between "good touch" and "bad touch." They may see sexual abuse as punishment for sinful thoughts or actions and blame themselves for it.

For example, in one case when a mother was told by her daughter that she was being abused by male relatives, she slapped her daughter for having "bad ideas." Her first reaction was to place the blame on the child. Later the woman disclosed that she had been sexually abused at the onset of puberty. Because at that time, when she was beginning to have thoughts about sex and curiosity about men, she believed the abuse was a punishment for these "bad" thoughts. Her interpretation for her own abuse carried over to her feelings about her daughter's abuse.

Later, she was able to clarify for herself that her thoughts and her daughter's thoughts did not make bad things happen and that the abusers were responsible for their actions.

Denial In Native Communities

Many factors combine to strengthen the atmosphere of denial in Native families where incest or child sexual abuse is

occurring. Unfortunately, denial is a defense mechanism that
allows the abuse to continue.

Contributing Factors

The Force of Habit

The habit of denial can develop in response to the pervasive
and devastating impact of alcohol on Native families. (I discuss
this problem in much greater detail below in *Dually Affected
Families*.)

Children who grow up in a home where one or more parents
is chemically addicted live by rules (identified by Dr. Claudia
Black (1982) as "Don't Talk, Don't Feel, Don't Trust") that support
and reinforce delusion and denial. In order to survive, children
adapt to the dysfunction around them by denying that it exists.

These children unconsciously carry these rules and the
subsequent coping behavior into their adult lives where they
continue to impact their work, private lives, families, friends and
communities, often with devastating effect.

Loyalty to the Community

The historical experience of Native people makes them very
reluctant to reveal sexual abuse problems to outsiders. Fear of
bringing in alien, outside *white* others creates pressure to keep
the family secret. The R.C.M.P., social workers, (who are often
seen as "baby stealers"), and the legal justice system can all be
seen as oppressors rather than helpers. The victim may be torn
between her desire for the abuse to end, and feelings of loyalty
towards her own people. This is slowly changing due to public
education within the Native community with social workers and
the R.C.M.P.

Fear of Gossip

In other cases, the fear of gossip and lack of confidentiality has
served to keep individuals from disclosing to professionals who
come from the community. This fear can be aggravated by family
or other alliances.

Also, because of the reality of the extended family in Native
communities, the number of individuals affected by the incest,
and the pressure on the victim to deny that it has occurred, can be
greater. The family circle might include the victim(s), non-
offending parent, the offender, aunts, uncles, nieces, nephews
and grandparents. All or any combination of these family
members may have shared the same dwelling over a period of
years.

If denial is present throughout this extended circle, the victim is faced with tremendous pressure not to disclose her abuse, and if she does reveal it, to recant later.

Group Denial

Sometimes helpers will encounter entire communities that are aware, at some level, that sexual abuse is occurring but are denying it at the same time. Consider the following statement by a victim.

"I was really scared to tell anyone about what had happened to me. I knew that after I told, something bad would happen. When I told a worker what had happened they talked to my mom and dad about it, and my dad said I was lying. After they found out they wouldn't talk to me any more, and the people within my community wouldn't talk to me neither. Before telling anybody about what my dad did it still felt like I didn't belong. Nobody in my community wanted to hear about sexual abuse and I think that no one was open to listening to it."

This comes from a letter written by a fifteen year old girl who, prior to disclosure, felt alienated not only from her family, but from the community as a whole. She indicated in counselling that she believed the community was not willing and ready to hear about the sexual abuse that was occurring within it. As a result she saw herself as ostracized and pushed away, even before disclosure occurred.

After disclosure, the worker she had informed was not prepared to deal with the allegation of sexual abuse and was not supported by council or the community in respect to helping this child. Consequently, the child was told to forget the issue as she would create problems not only for herself and family but for the community as well. This confirmed her original beliefs and increased her emotional pain.

In cases such as this, once the "community's secret" has been broken, and group denial is no longer possible, helpers must be sensitive to the pain that the whole community may be feeling.

Socialization

Sometimes the mother (or other female members of the family) has suffered from sexual abuse and sees it as "a woman's lot." She probably has blocked and denied the pain around her own abuse and does not want to, or cannot feel her child's pain.

Also, if incest has been occurring for three generations in a family, many members may have internalized a concept of "this is how it is."

"Spiritual" Connections to Denial

For many reasons, including the historical circumstances which surround the question of traditional Native spirituality, dealing with "spiritual" connections to abuse is extremely sensitive. However, as we saw in the chapter addressing the characteristics of the offender, hiding behind or manipulating spiritual beliefs can become a strong defense for the offender, especially when people become very cautious of challenging another's behaviors. In such cases, it can be helpful if we remind ourselves that it is the offense we are confronting, not the spiritual beliefs.

For example, a man who was recognized as an Elder, and who conducted traditional sweatlodge ceremonies, was discovered to be touching some of the children attending these functions. His actions in regard to molesting these children were not the result of his spiritual beliefs, but members of his community were terrified to confront him because of his position and status. Their denial of the sexual abuse, therefore, was prompted by fear.

There have also been incidents in Native situations when a child victim's symptoms of abuse such as crying, clinging to the non-offending parent, nightmares, acting out etc. have been attributed to "bad medicine" (the result of someone having "cursed" the child.)

In one case, a five year old child was being consistently molested when she was left with her grandfather. Her mother, who had also been molested by him as a child, said that her daughter's behaviors and vaginal discharge were the result of Bad Medicine which her ex-husband was directing at her daughter for reasons of vengeance.

In this situation, we see denial and rationalizing by the mother as a means of protecting herself against her own pain and the sense of powerlessness in having to deal with her own abuse and that of her daughter, by the same man. Since she was helpless as a child, the reoccurrence of the same situation probably *feels* like a curse.

This issue, of symptoms being attributed to a negative use of spiritual power, is also highly sensitive. A helper who deals with this will have to clarify his or her own beliefs and emotions prior to responding. It is highly likely that a non-Native person would be challenged if he or she disputed the claim.

In all cases where someone is faced with abuse which has a "spiritual" component or justification, it would be useful to seek out several individuals who are knowledgeable about Native spirituality. It is important to remember that these people may have varying opinions about the same situation. Hearing about the beliefs of others can assist us in clarifying our own.

Dually Affected Families:
Substance Abuse and People Abuse

A dually affected family is one in which both substances abuse (alcohol, drugs, inhalents) and people abuse are occurring. The incidence of both kinds of abuse being present in Native families is high. Therefore, it is important for helpers to understand the relationship between the two in order to move the family into recovery.

Alcoholism

It has been said that Native people are 100% affected by alcoholism. This means that somewhere within the family circle, someone is an alcoholic. The remaining individuals are "affected" by the disease even if they are not drinking.

The definition of an alcoholic referred to here is the generally used one, which states that the person is an alcoholic or addict when the use of alcohol and/or other drugs interferes in any significant area of a person's life, and he or she continues to use alcohol and/or drugs in spite of the consequences. The consequences include damage to the emotional, physical, mental and spiritual health of the individual.

Although they are linked, sexual abuse and substance abuse consist of separate, distinct behaviors or actions; tipping a bottle to your mouth is not the same as touching a child's vagina. Both actions, although they involve very different choices, may stem from similar feelings: loneliness, fear, worthlessness. Both kinds of behavior fail to resolve the problems or meet the real needs of the individuals involved.

Helpers who are working with sexual abuse in Native communities need to familiarize themselves with substance abuse treatment. It will be necessary for them to learn about the issues, explore the resources available in their area, and research referral methods and treatment centers that specialize in Native clientele. In addition, they should learn about the theories subscribed to in these treatment centers such as the Disease Concept of Alcoholism, and the twelve steps within the treatment program offered by Alcoholics Anonymous.

Because alcohol and drugs act to lower inhibitions, we often witness or hear about extreme kinds of people abuse in Native communities. It is important that this is not interpreted as a cultural norm or construed to fit the myth of the "ignorant savage." Sometimes the Native Community's lack of knowledge and resources to deal with these extremes is interpreted as condoning attitudes which support this myth.

Often, if an individual abuses a child or other people only when he has been drinking, he will excuse his behavior by saying that it is a result of the drinking. This helps the offender to avoid responsibility for his actions and enables him to continue the abuse. Sometimes an offender will drink or use drugs as an excuse to touch a child sexually. In any case, the offender employs a wide range of defense mechanisms to justify his abuse of both substances and people. A few examples are given below.

Some Defense Mechanisms Operating in Dually Affected Families

	Substance Abuse	Sexual Abuse
Minimizing	"I only had a couple of drinks."	"I only touched her a couple of times."
Blaming	"If my boss would get off my back I wouldn't drink."	"If my wife wasn't such a nag, I wouldn't have to turn to my child."
Rationalizing	"A few drinks helps calm my nerves and then I don't yell at anyone."	"My child and I both need affection and touching. Parents need to teach their own children about sex."

Many people believe that if a person stops drinking the sexual abuse will end. Although this isn't necessarily true, sobriety is the environment necessary to permit progress in working on the other behaviors. Ideally, an offender needs treatment for both the abusive behaviors. However, **it is essential that the substance abuse is treated first.**

If an offender begins to receive treatment for sexual abuse prior to gaining sobriety he will not be able to resolve his issues around these behaviors because the alcohol or drugs serve to block emotions. Dealing with the emotional issues, is at the core of understanding why the sexual abuse was occurring.

This points to a need for increased dialogue among workers from the areas of alcohol and addictions, and sexual abuse and family violence,   and for improved coordination of   their intervention and treatment goals.

The treatment indications for a dually affected family are:

1. Separate the individuals and get everyone to safety.

2. Begin treatment for the substance abuse.
3. Stabilize the sobriety.
4. Begin treatment for the sexual abuse.
5. Aftercare.

If other members of the family such as the victim, non-offending spouse or siblings are also abusing substances, they also need to gain sobriety before they can deal with the sexual abuse. Individuals within the family should not enter the same addictions treatment center at the same time, however, as their issues around the abuse will interfere with their goal of gaining sobriety.

Finally, it is important for all the family members to receive education about alcoholism and addictions, even if they are not abusing substances themselves. They need to examine and explore their own attitudes and feelings about addictions in a supportive environment such as counselling or treatment. Al-anon and Al-ateen programs which work from the Twelve Step program, can also provide support.

It is also essential for all the members of families impacted by alcoholism to understand the difference between enabling behaviors (those which protect the user from the harmful consequences of his actions), and non-enabling behaviors (those which allow the user to experience the results of his choices).

Children of Alcoholics (C.O.A's)

Recently C.O.A.'s have been identified as a group of individuals who share many common characteristics, emotions and behaviors. For example, as adults, they run an increased risk of becoming an alcoholic, or marrying one. (Dr. Black)

When we examine the past events of children who grew up in a dysfunctional family, we find that they have suffered many losses ranging from the very real visible ones such as Christmas celebrations, birthdays, pets, friends and loved ones, to less tangible ones such as dignity, joy, safety and peace.

Often these children have never had a chance or place to grieve these losses. They have "stuffed" their sadness in an attempt to survive and cope. As adults, they still carry the sadness but do not understand its source. To be healed, they need to grieve, to do the emotional work necessary to release the pain and reach peace.

Many people have been assisted through treatment and the support of special groups offered through "Adult Children of Alcoholics" (A.C.O.A.'s). New literature is available on the subject which can provide knowledge and awareness.

Inhalent Abuse: A Special Case

The abuse of inhalents (gas, glue, solvents etc.) through "sniffing" or "huffing" can lead to permanent irreversible brain damage. The severity of brain disorders among inhalent abusers depends on the substance (or combination of substances) being abused and the length and frequency of use.

Because children who abuse inhalents, run an extremely high risk of organic brain disorders, they usually require specialized treatment. Some of them must be stabilized with drugs which can be prescribed only by a competent psychiatrist.

At the present time there are no treatment models in North America to borrow or learn from in dealing with the problem of inhalent abuse; the whole area is new and uncharted. Traditional addictions treatment centers are hard pressed to find the staff or training to deal with the special needs of inhalent abusers. However, for now, they provide the only treatment available.

Research into the problem is presently being conducted by the National Native Treatment Director of Solvents and Abuse (1988).

The Untreated Professional

Workers who grew up in an alcoholic or otherwise dysfunctional home, (A.C.O.A.'s), need to clarify how this experience affects their roles as professionals. They have learned patterns of co-dependency and caring for others. This may be the reason they are attracted to the role of caregiver as an adult.

If they are untreated for their own pain and losses experienced in childhood, they will experience many problems in dealing with the issues they must face through their role as a professional. Low self-esteem, high expectations, an inability to establish clear limits or boundaries, confusing and overwhelming feelings of powerlessness, frustration and anger are all issues which may surface in work-related situations and may need to be examined.

Untreated A.C.O.A.'s live with a dread of loss of control in themselves and others and may be over controlling as a way of compensating. Also, they often have difficulty maintaining a clear sense of self and can easily become enmeshed in others' problems. Only by working through and resolving their own problems related to childhood experiences, will they achieve health for themselves, and effectiveness in assisting others to health.

Conclusion

The relationship of substance abuse and people abuse is a new area that is still being charted.

The challenge for people working in Native communities is to continue to explore and search for solutions which encompass these two dynamics. We cannot ethically or morally ignore their co-existence.

Healing will increase as the problems are identified, the silence is broken and the dialogue begins between members of the various professions which address these issues.

This challenge points to hope and a new life in recovery. As yesterday's child finds wholeness and health, the future of tomorrow's children is secured.

Chapter 12
Where To From Here?
Developing Effective Treatment Programs for Sexual Abuse in Native Communities
by Maggie Hodgson

Our people are in our midnight.
We'll come into our daylight and become leaders,
when the eagle lands on the moon.

Hopi Prophecy circa 1850

Introduction

Since it was made, this prophecy has been handed down by Natives from generation to generation even though they did not know what it meant. Finally, on July 20, 1969, when astronauts landed on the moon, the message they sent back to earth was: "The Eagle has landed."

In that week, the first Native alcohol program opened up in North America. These programs have been the leaders in bringing us out of our midnight of residential schools, alcoholism and family breakdown. Our people are losing their sense of powerlessness, and actively changing substance abuse problems.

The prophecy carries on even in the writing of this book, and in the growth of community spirit aimed at solving sexual abuse problems afflicting Native communities.

For years, to our great disadvantage, we have accepted three rules of denial ("Don't Talk, Don't Feel, Don't Trust.") identified by Dr. Black.

Using these, we have tried to close up and hide the sexual abuse issue: we have tried to *envelop* the problem. Now we must choose the opposite road: to open it up, and *develop* treatment approaches.

The need to treat sexual abuse problems is identified everywhere by care givers in the Native community. Band Social Workers, alcohol workers, Community Health Representatives (C.H.R.'s) and school counsellors are not only hearing disclosures of sexual abuse from the youth in their communities, they also see its symptoms: depression, suicide, dysfunctional school behavior, juvenile delinquency, and promiscuity.

If we truly want to deal with the pain of our children's spirit, we must develop effective sexual abuse treatment programs. To succeed in the Native community, these programs must be community-based. Yet, the multifaceted issues of caregivers, families, and community grieving can seriously inhibit the effective development of a such an approach.

This chapter tries to highlight some of the cultural factors requiring careful consideration if programs to treat sexual abuse problems in Native communities are to meet with the greatest possible success.

Beyond Sobriety

Alcoholism has been the most visible sign of dysfunction in our communities and has received the most attention from both Government and Native communities.

The growing success of the 8 year old National Native Alcohol and Drug Abuse Program (NNADAP) is resulting in more Native service givers being in the helping profession.

As substance abuse is reduced, violence and sexual abuse issues become more prominent. These problems existed while there was excessive drinking, of course, but they were often not talked about because people believed the myth that the alcohol was *causing* these other forms of abuse. As the alcohol is removed, violence and sexual abuse issues must be dealt with, not only for their own sake, but also to help stabilize the newfound sobriety; recovering Native alcoholics are more likely to relapse if they are untreated for the violence and/or sexual abuse they have experienced.

Some communities which have succeeded in developing a high rate of sobriety (85%-95%), experience an increase in the number of disclosures of child sexual abuse. Therefore, the planners of programs to drastically reduce alcoholism should also set up treatment plans to deal with an increase in sexual abuse reports.

One such community has sweat lodge ceremonies, a sexual abuse survivors peer group, adult children of alcoholics group, alcoholics anonymous groups, community feasts, Al-anon groups, youth groups and training as their community-based approach to dealing with violence. They are effectively breaking the three rules which have kept them powerless for so long, by building a foundation of *talking* and *trust* in which people can deal with their *feelings*. Although that process has taken 10 years, and they still have many obstacles to overcome, this community has made substantial progress in moving their community social system towards health.

Another Native community which has moved from 100%

alcoholism to 85% sobriety, has a very strong Al-ateen group, a youth drama group, an Alcoholics Anonymous group, mobile treatment and sexual abuse therapy for families. They are presently utilizing 3 therapists from urban areas who come to their communities to assist sexual abuse survivors. Meanwhile, they are planning a protocol system for disclosures, and training for their on-reserve service givers. This community, still in the early stages of development, has accomplished this in three years.

Extended Families: "Greatest Strength/Greatest Weakness"

In referring to our extended families, Elder Abe Burnstick, now deceased, said: "For many of us, our greatest strength is our greatest weakness."

The wisdom of this statement is clearly seen when a Native victim of sexual abuse discloses the problem. If extended family members are involved, loyalty to the perpetrator often results in the sexual abuse not being reported.

If our extended families are truly to be our greatest strength and *not* our greatest weakness, we *must* report abuse. Only by doing so will the perpetrators receive treatment to become healthy members of the family and feel good about themselves. Only through treatment can we ensure that they will not offend again, and that the child victims and all future children who could be potentially abused will be protected. Then our "greatest strength", our extended families, will truly be our greatest strength.

Grieving In Native Communities

Grieving is another issue that affects Native communities and care givers. Due to high rates of alcoholism, violence, death, separations and children going to care, many people in our communities become locked in the anger stage of grieving. A sense of powerlessness becomes pervasive and people become "other-directed" with their anger. They blame the Chief and Council, government, or other clans. Agencies blame each other for the collective pain in the community, and everyone mistrusts everyone else.

Because Native communities are often small, pandemic grieving issues can have depressive effects on all the residents. These can potentially hinder the setting up of an effective treatment program or a protocol system for receiving and responding to disclosures of child sexual abuse in a healthy manner. It is important, therefore, if child sexual abuse is to be dealt with effectively, that program planners acknowledge the many grieving issues in the community.

Cooperative Process-Shared Responsibility

If the community is to help people work through the *don't trust* rule into developing a *trust* rule, the treatment programs they set up must utilize both existing local resources and assistance from provincially funded outside treatment programs for offenders and their families. This is not to suggest that those provincial programs must be delivered in the Native community. They can assist by training local people to develop their own treatment programs, or by jointly operating programs.

Whatever strategy is undertaken, there must be *mutual respect* between the government agency and Native community when setting up treatment programs.

It is imperative also, that the non-Native professional who plans to assist a Native community to develop a child sexual abuse treatment program, gain an appreciation of the *collective thought* or sense of community mindedness which exists in Native communities, given the extended family system. Understanding how community mindedness can be harnessed to support the effort of care givers can increase the probability of success of any program.

Communities Affected by Multiple Charges of Sexual Abuse

Due to the smallness of most Native communities, it is difficult to effectively maintain confidentiality for complainants in situations where there are many charges laid against a perpetrator. Even if the care givers honor the confidentiality of the complainant, usually the extended families are so angry that they discuss the victimization of their relative with community members.

In one Native community, there was tremendous anger directed against a perpetrator who faced more than ten charges of sexual abuse. A major split developed in the community as the friends and relatives of the perpetrator took sides against the friends and relatives of the victims. There being no therapy program available in the immediate vicinity, the whole community became locked into shock, grief and pain.

This community is now actively seeking funds to assist young people affected by the abuse that was disclosed, and for many other disclosures which surfaced because of the notoriety of the initial case.

In another community, a large number of charges have been laid against a former residential school dorm supervisor. Here an on-site therapist is helping victims deal with the trauma of long term sexual abuse suffered in residential school.

Many former residential school residents who have been the victims of sexual abuse feel caught between their own need to get well and the old laws of respecting "Father" or "Sister" who were their surrogate parents/caretakers during that era. The reluctance of the Churches, which operated the schools, to acknowledge and assist the Native community members who have suffered physical and sexual abuse there, compounds the difficulty of building effective treatment programs.

Community anger about the general victimization of students within the residential school system clouds the treatment issues for the victims. In some cases, members of two or three generations of a given family were abused in residential schools. Grieving of cultural loss becomes a treatment issue for the whole community when these multi-charge situations arise.

In general, multiple charges of sexual abuse give rise to even more disclosures of sexual abuse by victims within the community. This is an important consideration for planners.

Issues for Native Care Givers

Recognizing that their lack of information prevents them from making effective interventions in sexual abuse cases, Band Social Workers, alcohol workers, C.H.R.'s and school counsellors are all seeking more information on child sexual abuse. They are starting to bring in resources to conduct workshops on signs and symptoms of child sexual abuse. Our experience to date in setting up such workshops has revealed a number of difficult problems faced by Native care givers working in this field.

Care Giver/Care Receiver

Ideally, people in any human services field will have already been treated, or not need treatment for the problems they are working with.

Unfortunately, due to the relatively recent development of sobriety in many of our communities, this ideal is often not the reality (as of 1988). It is only within the last few years that there have been more professionally trained Native people entering the field.

In many of our communities, virtually 100% of our population has been affected by alcoholism, either directly or indirectly. People raised in homes impacted by alcoholism, were usually subjected to physical and/or sexual abuse. This means that all of us have been affected, either personally or through an immediate or extended family member.

In the case of sexual abuse, the extent of the problem in Native communities has been hidden through the *don't talk* rule. How effectively this has been done often becomes apparent when a "Signs and Symptoms" workshop is given for care givers working in any branch of the human services field.

Generally, care givers come to the workshops in the best interest of their "clients" so that they are able to identify and support sexually abused children. Although the workshops initially focus on "those children", inevitably many workshop participants disclose that they are survivors of past abuse, either sexual or physical. Therefore, in running sexual abuse workshops, it is important to have already identified local resources where these "care givers/victims" might attend counselling for themselves.

Prior Assessment

In matters of treating sexual abuse, serious consideration should be given to the clinical assessment of local care givers in order to ensure that their own treatment is set up prior to the development of a program which aims to help them assist others. This will protect the well being of both the care giver and the client.

Some Native care givers/victims have been or are in therapy, and others should be. Yet many who need it are reluctant to seek it because of the attitude that Alcohol Counsellors, Band C.H.R.'s, and Band Social Workers should be well, and not in need of therapy if they are counselling others. This often places the worker in a double bind, that of needing therapy, and yet feeling unable to admit it and seek it.

As with other victims of sexual abuse, care givers/victims are fearful of the consequences of disclosing their abuse. Frequently, the abuser is an immediate relative or friend of the family, and may be still an active perpetrator.

Workshop participants may also be reluctant to disclose abuse out of a sense of shame, or fear of social or family isolation, even if the abuse took place 5 to 20 years earlier. They also may fear physical recrimination from the perpetrator or members of his extended family.

Care givers/victims must be assisted in setting up self care plans which include therapy. If a treatment program is developed, the community based service giver and the outside resource must ensure a strong peer support system for the Native service giver even if the service giver is in active treatment.

In one Indian Band, the employee assistance program includes the attendance of all Band employees affected by physical violence or sexual abuse at *regular* therapy sessions. Another urban Native program includes the referral to therapy of all employees who are survivors of abuse. A certain amount of company time is allocated to them to attend therapy sessions regularly.

Treatment Problems Facing Care Givers/Victims

Emotional Turmoil and "Burnout"

The emotional turmoil experienced by untreated care givers/victims complicates every aspect of their attempts to deliver care to other victims or offenders who need help, even to the point that the care giver/victim's intervention does more harm than good.

For example, sometimes, Native care givers/victims working in the field of sexual abuse say "I cry for those children." Although this may be true in some cases, in many others, they cry for their own unresolved pain. Their rage towards the offender or the child victim's mother may in part be rage at the offender who abused them as a child, or at their own mothers who they may feel did not protect them from the abuse.

In addition, the "burn-out" that is often complained about in the Native human service field, is not always due to high case loads; it sometimes results from the emotional, physical and spiritual stress experienced by care givers/victims whose pain from their own past abuse is unresolved.

Cases Within the Extended Family

The biggest issue facing the community based service giver is pressure from the extended family not to report abuse within that family system. In some situations, Native care givers are faced with the problem of dealing with disclosures of sexual abuse in which the perpetrator is a member of the care giver's extended family. This situation greatly increases the stress felt by both the care giver and the person making the disclosure.

In the non-Native community, the service giver can often

transfer immediate family cases to another worker, quit, move to another area or refer the case to another agency. These choices are not available to Native service givers, since they have been raised in their community, are often raising their own children there, and plan to remain in their communities.

Matters of Trust

Care givers also face difficult choices when sexual abuse is disclosed by child victims who do not want anything done about it. They do not want the perpetrator to go to jail because he is a family member or another person in the community.

The *don't talk* rule must be broken in these cases because, in the best interest of the child victim, the abuse must stop. Both child welfare laws and the criminal code say the abuse must be reported. Native care givers who are receiving the disclosures and are in therapy or are untreated, find it difficult to break the *don't trust* rule. However, as difficult as it may be, care givers must do what is necessary to protect these children who have risked disclosure. Children must not feel betrayed once again by adults they trust. If nothing is done, these children will respond by pulling into themselves and will become more alone with their anger, pain, guilt and shame.

Abuse by Elderly Offenders

Another very difficult situation faces Native care givers when the abuser is an elderly person in the community. On the one hand, the cultural norm is to respect older people and to protect them. But on the other, the care giver must protect the innocent victims of the abuse. Due to their sense of powerlessness about their own having been abused as a child, untreated Native care givers/victims may not see the alternatives open to deal with the disclosure about the family abuse in a legally correct manner. It is important to assist them in identifying the possibilities of treatment, not only for the victim, but also for the offender.

Spirituality

It is helpful, when designing workshops or treatment programs on sexual abuse, to build a spiritual and cultural component into the program. Acknowledgement of the harm to the spirit of the individual, extended family and community lends itself to reinforcing the "spirit of community mindedness" which can help the program succeed.

Within our communities, we have many active faiths; but, even given this reality, it is still possible to find a common ground on which to start sessions with a sense of spirit without imposing one's faith in the process. Elders and legends such as the Hopi Prophecy can be the basis for this important component within our reinforcing hope, self-love and mutual respect in our communities.

Conclusion

The Hopi prophecy with which I began this chapter, promises that we shall emerge from our midnight into daylight and become leaders. The progress we have made towards establishing and maintaining sobriety among our people, is an important first step. The next one, is dealing with the problem of sexual abuse within our communities.

To do this, we must draw upon the resources of provincially funded programs and non-Native therapists. Working with them, in a spirit of *mutual* respect, we can develop the community-based programs we need, programs which address the essential issues of Native communities.

We must begin by abandoning the three rules of denial, and by acknowledging collective grief and the issues of care givers/victims.

When we have done this, and made the extended family our truly greatest strength, we shall emerge from our midnight into daylight, becoming the leaders we are capable of being.

Glossary

adult - a person seventeen years of age or older.

child - a person under the age of seventeen years.

child sexual abuse/child sexual assault - any sexual exploitation of a child by an adult or someone perceived by the child to be more powerful or dominant than they. Such exploitation may include fondling, intercourse, oral or anal sex, exposure to sexually related acts or materials, or verbal suggestions.

coerce - the exertion of power, whether it is physical, psychological, mental, or moral, over another.

dually affected families - a family where both substance abuse and sexual abuse are occurring. It is suggested that the combination of substance abuse and child abuse is very high in Native communities, 85%-95% in some cases. (We are still at a stage of exploration and discovery in regards to the relationship between the two forms of abuse.)

extended families - a network of individuals acting in a primary relationship with another individual. This can consist of blood relatives, but also significant others such as in-laws or persons who fulfill the same role. In traditional Native culture, a person can "adopt" someone if they feel there is a "spiritual kinship" between them. Afterwards, this person may be called "sister, brother, uncle, aunt, father, mother, grandmother, grandfather, daughter, son, niece, nephew, granddaughter, or grandson."

force - see **coerce**

inappropriate sexual contact - includes molestation, fondling, intercourse, oral/genital contact, sodomy, coercing or tricking or bribing a child to pose for photos or videos involving sexual acts, coercing a child to do pornography or view sexually explicit material, coercing nudity, coercing a child to listen to or hear explicit depictions of sexual acts or violence, threats of sexual contact or violence, bestiality, sexual sadism or torture.

incest - any sexual involvement between blood relatives, blended family members, step-relatives, or by people who view their relationship with that person as a member of an immediate or extended family. The sexual involvement may include anything listed under **inappropriate sexual contact** above.

incest offender - someone who may be sexually involved with children but whose sexual orientation is for people of or about the same age as himself/herself.

manipulation - physically, emotionally or psychologically influencing someone, either directly or indirectly, to act in a way wanted by the manipulator.

Native - any Canadian individual of aboriginal descent. This includes status and non-status Indians, Inuit, Dene, Inuvialiut, and Metis (mixed blood or half breeds).

non-offending parent - except when otherwise specified, this will refer to the mother or female partner in a relationship.

nuclear family - a family group that consists only of father, mother and children.

offender - except when otherwise specified, this will refer to an adult male who has committed either incest or child sexual abuse.

parent - a person, male or female, in the role of providing guardianship. The person may have assumed this position or role either biologically, through marriage or partnership.

pedophile - a person who, either in act or fantasy, has an exclusive or primary sexual attraction to children.

reserve - (short for reservation) a tract of land allotted by the Crown to Indians who have signed a treaty in exchange for specific rights.

sibling - except when otherwise specified, this will refer to the natural brother or sister, or step-brother or step-sister of the victim.

victim - except when otherwise specified, this will refer to a female child under the age of seventeen years.